You've Got a Point!

STUNNING QUILTS WITH TRIANGLE-IN-A-SQUARE BLOCKS

Anna Dineen

Martingale®
Create with Confidence

You've Got a Point! Stunning Quilts with
Triangle-in-a-Square Blocks
© 2022 by Anna Dineen

Martingale®
18939 120th Ave. NE, Ste. 101
Bothell, WA 98011-9511 USA
ShopMartingale.com

Printed in Hong Kong
27 26 25 24 23 22   8 7 6 5 4 3 2 1

Library of Congress Cataloging-in-Publication Data is available upon request.

ISBN: 978-1-68356-194-1

MISSION STATEMENT

We empower makers who use fabric and yarn to make life more enjoyable.

CREDITS

PRESIDENT AND
CHIEF VISIONARY OFFICER
Jennifer Erbe Keltner

CONTENT DIRECTOR
Karen Costello Soltys

DESIGN MANAGER
Adrienne Smitke

TECHNICAL EDITOR
Nancy Mahoney

PRODUCTION MANAGER
Regina Girard

COPY EDITOR
Sheila Chapman Ryan

COVER AND
BOOK DESIGNER
Mia Mar

ILLUSTRATOR
Sandy Loi

PHOTOGRAPHERS
Adam Albright
Brent Kane

SPECIAL THANKS
Photography for this book was taken at:
The home of Jodi Allen in Woodinville, Washington
The home of Tracy Fish in Kenmore, Washington
Happy Hollow Farm in Silvana, Washington
The home of Julie Smiley in Des Moines, Iowa

DEDICATION

To my grandmothers, Shelby Hayes and Ann Porter, and the precious memories I have of them sharing their love of crafting with me and teaching me the foundations of sewing and needlework.

Contents

Introduction

Fun fact: The very first quilt pattern I ever designed, Double Time, featured triangle-in-a-square units, but I'd never actually *made* a triangle-in-a-square unit prior to making that quilt. I had just started working at Moda Fabrics and suddenly had access to tools I'd never seen or tried before. I saw a Bloc Loc Triangle in a Square Ruler Set and thought, "I bet I could do something fun with that!" It really *was* fun to try a new tool and a new technique.

Some months later, as part of a fabric showcase for Jera Brandvig's Loyal Heights fabric collection, I designed my second original quilt pattern. This design also happened to feature triangle-in-a-square units—albeit modified into diamond-in-a-rectangle units. (That pattern, Queens Road, is happily featured in this book on page 65.)

About a year after that, I found myself tinkering with another original design and—*quelle surprise*—triangle-in-a-square units found their way into that pattern as well. I had a lightbulb moment: Clearly, I had a thing for this particular technique! I'd designed three totally different quilts featuring triangle-in-a-square units . . . how many more unique patterns could I create? That felt like a great challenge to set for myself, and I'm thrilled to be able to share the results with you here in this book.

We all quilt for different reasons: to make tangible gifts of love for family and friends, to take our minds off of the day-to-day grind, to have an excuse to buy (hoard) and play with pretty fabric, to channel the spirits of creative women (and men) who came before us, or a combination of all of the above and more. Regardless of the reasons that spur us to sit at our sewing machines for hours at a time, what I love the most about the actual mechanics of quilting is the seemingly limitless opportunities to push and hone our technical skills through new techniques, new blocks, and new construction methods.

If you're a beginning quilter or you've never made a triangle-in-a-square unit before, I hope this book inspires you to tackle a new technique. My goal is to demystify the construction for you. And if you've made plenty of these blocks before, I hope the patterns here offer a fresh take on them that will inspire you to make a few more.

Thank you for adding *You've Got a Point* to your quilting bookshelf. I hope that my designs will yield many happy returns on your investment.

Cheers!

Making Triangle-in-a-Square Units

In his book *Outliers*, Malcom Gladwell proposes that it takes 10,000 hours of practice to become an expert in something. In the course of making this book, I've made probably 1,500 triangle-in-a-square units. That's a far cry from 10,000 hours, but it's still enough to figure out some best practices for achieving a measure of consistency in my results, which I'm sharing with you to spare you from having to make thousands of your own—unless you just want to, and who am I to stop you? (In case you're wondering, there are 1,144 triangle-in-a-square units in the patterns in this book.)

Regardless of the finished size or color combinations, triangle-in-a-square units open up new design possibilities for your patchwork.

Specialty rulers have been a game-changer in the quilting world. Gone are the days when our only option was to trace and cut out our own templates from cardboard or template plastic. Instead, we can choose from an incredible range of sturdy and accurate rulers that help us cut just about any size and shape we can think of.

Choosing a Ruler Set

While you can find a variety of rulers and tools, let's take a look at the two most popular ruler sets for making triangle units: Bloc Loc Triangle in a Square Ruler Sets and the Wrights EZ Quilting Tri-Recs Tool set.

Bloc Loc Triangle in a Square Ruler Sets

If you've been quilting for a bit, you've likely heard of Bloc Loc rulers. Bloc Loc makes an array of rulers in all sizes and shapes, from utilitarian half-square triangle and flying-geese rulers to sets for specialty blocks and units such as kite-in-a-square, pineapple, kaleidoscope, and triangle-in-a-square. The defining feature is a unique groove into which a seam allowance fits neatly and snugly, making for more confident and accurate trimming. The groove locks the ruler in place on the block or unit, preventing slips and accidental slices into the unit. I heartily recommend a rotary-cutting glove to prevent more painful slices. (Ask me how I know.)

Each Bloc Loc specialty ruler is a specific size, which means that investing in a 4" finished triangle-in-a-square ruler set will give you the templates to

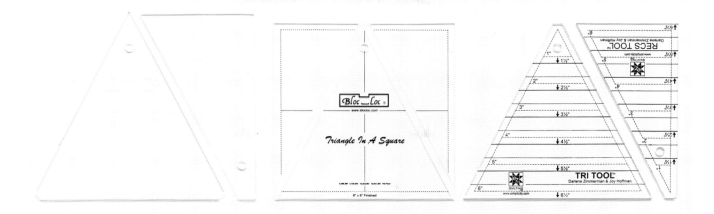

The Bloc Loc Triangle in a Square Ruler Set (left and center) comes with three pieces: two triangles for cutting the shapes and one ruler for trimming the units to size. The Tri-Recs Tool Set (right) has two pieces to cut the two different types of triangles needed.

make 4" finished triangle units only. What you get in return for your investment, however, is a Mary Poppins block—practically perfect in every way. Bloc Loc rulers are designed so that the *unfinished* unit is ½" larger than it needs to be, giving you lots of wiggle room to trim to the size you need. I have yet to make a block or unit using my Bloc Loc rulers that didn't make me look like a better sewist than I actually am.

A Bloc Loc Triangle in a Square Ruler Set contains three pieces—the center triangle cutting template, the side triangle cutting template, and the grooved ruler for trimming the block or unit. The patterns in this book feature finished 2", 3", 4", and 6" triangle units. The ruler sets are sold by finished size, which are 1½", 2", 3", 4", and 6" square, so read the materials list closely to make sure you get the correct ruler set for the pattern you want to make.

If you're a beginning quilter or are still working on consistent fabric cutting and a perfect ¼" seam allowance, I recommend investing in either the 2" or 4" Bloc Loc Ruler Set first, for a couple of reasons. On one hand, half of the patterns in this book feature 2" triangle units, so you'll get the most bang for your buck with that size. Additionally, I've found that when sewing 2" triangle units in particular, I appreciate the extra fabric buffer that Bloc Loc's trim-down approach provides. On the other hand, the Queens Road pattern (page 65) is specifically written for the 4" ruler set, so you'll definitely need that set when you're ready to make a Queens Road quilt.

Wrights EZ Quilting Tri-Recs Tool Set

Whereas the Bloc Loc ruler uses more fabric to give you practically perfect results for just one unit size, the EZ Quilting Tri-Recs Tool set is a more versatile set for more efficient fabric use and for making blocks and units in a wide range of sizes. However, this ruler set requires a little more practice and consistent sewing to achieve uniform results.

Together, the Tri Tool and the Recs Tool comprise the Tri-Recs set. These acrylic cutting templates are marked with guidelines from 1" to 6½", so with one ruler set, you could make triangle units for every quilt in this book.

From a fabric usage standpoint, the Tri-Recs Tool is more efficient because you'll cut your fabric exactly to size. For example, cutting center and side triangles from a 3½"-wide fabric strip makes triangle units that measure 3½" square, including seam allowances. Less fabric to trim away means less fabric waste—but it also means there's less margin for error.

That being said, I still recommend getting the Tri-Recs set if you can get only one ruler set. It requires less fabric and is versatile enough to make every quilt but one in this book, which appeals to the pragmatist in me!

Seeing Is Believing

I've given you my ruler recommendations, but which one did *I* use to make the quilts in this book? A hybrid of both, actually. I used the Tri-Recs tools to cut my center and side triangle pieces, and I used the grooved Bloc Loc rulers to trim my units.

Here you can see the difference that the Bloc Loc's oversized approach makes. Compare the triangle unit made with the Bloc Loc center and side triangle cutting templates. Notice how much fabric will end up being trimmed off!

The triangle unit on the right was made with the Tri-Recs tools. The result is a unit that's pretty much the correct unfinished size—very little fabric will be trimmed off.

Regardless of how much or how little fabric must be trimmed away, nothing beats that grooved Bloc Loc ruler for quick and accurate trimming—which is why I feel using both ruler sets offered the best of both worlds.

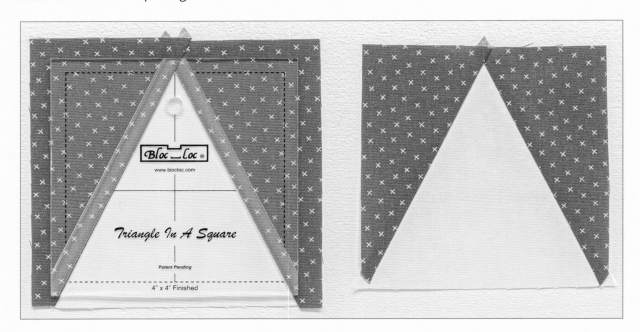

Bloc Loc vs. Tri-Recs at a Glance

Bloc Loc Ruler Set

• One ruler set produces one unit size only

• Requires more fabric

• Grooved ruler makes trimming easy

• Yields precisely sized, uniform blocks and units

Tri-Recs Tools

• Can be used to make finished blocks and units from 1" to 6"

• Uses less fabric

• No block ruler for trimming

• Takes practice to yield consistent results

A Word about Fabric Requirements

As I began writing the patterns for this book, I was faced with a dilemma. Should I calculate the fabric requirements and determine cutting instructions based on the specifications for the Tri-Recs set or each individual Bloc Loc set? Offering both sets of measurements for each pattern would have been confusing and made this book much longer than it needed to be.

For the sake of consistency and clarity, I've chosen to base the fabric requirements and cutting instructions for the patterns in this book on the Tri-Recs ruler (except for Queens Road on page 65, which is written specifically for using a Bloc Loc set). If you have or decide to purchase a Tri-Recs set, you can follow the fabric requirements and cutting instructions in this book exactly as they're given.

However—and this is important!—if you'd like to use a Bloc Loc set for any of the patterns besides Queens Road, you'll need to increase the amount of fabric used for the triangle units by about 25% to cover the additional fabric the Bloc Loc templates require.

"magic angle" (as the ruler designer calls it) on the side triangles. Either way, the function is the same. In the context of fabric cutting and block sewing, the primary difference between these two ruler sets is merely the *size* of the pieces you cut. For a 2" finished triangle unit, you'll cut 2½" center and side triangles using the Tri-Recs set, but you'll cut a 3" center triangle and 3⅛" side triangles using the Bloc Loc set.

The cutting instructions for the patterns in this book are written to take advantage of cutting from full width-of-fabric strips, which means you'll cut enough strips to yield the required total number of center triangles and side triangle pairs from those strips without having to cut from leftover bits here and there. For the best results and most efficient cutting, keep your strips folded in half just like the fabric comes off the bolt, and always start cutting triangles from the selvage end.

Center Triangles

The following instructions and illustrations feature the Tri-Recs Tool set.

1 Align the top of the Tri Tool with the top of your folded fabric strip, making sure the bottom of the strip is aligned with the marked line that corresponds to the *unfinished* size of your triangle unit. Cut along the left and right sides of the Tri Tool to release two center triangles.

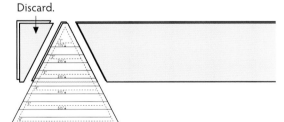

Discard.

Cutting the Triangles

The basic construction of a triangle unit is the same whether you use a Bloc Loc or Tri-Recs Ruler Set or you make your own templates. Every triangle unit is constructed from three pieces—a center triangle, a right-side triangle, and a left-side triangle. Both sets of templates feature small placement guides to help align the pieces for sewing.

For the Bloc Loc set, you'll trim the corners of the center triangle. For the Tri-Recs set, you'll cut the

2 Rotate the Tri Tool so that the tip is aligned with the bottom edge of the strip and the marked line that corresponds to the *unfinished* size of your triangle unit is aligned with the top of the strip. The left edge of the tool should be aligned with the angled edge of the strip. Cut along the right side of the Tri Tool to release two triangles.

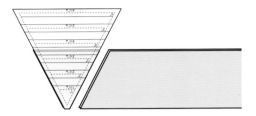

3 Repeat the process across the width of the strip. If needed, make straightening cuts as you go.

Side Triangles

For each triangle unit, you'll need a pair of side triangles—a left side and a right side—which are mirror images of each other. Cutting from a folded strip of fabric makes the process much easier. With one cut, you've released a matching pair of mirror-image triangles.

1 Align the top of the Recs Tool with the top of the folded strip, making sure the bottom of the strip is aligned with the marked line that corresponds to the unfinished size of your triangle unit. Cut along the left and right sides of the Recs Tool to release a pair of side triangles.

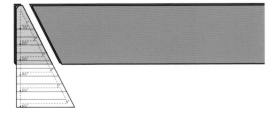

2 Without moving the Recs Tool, cut the "magic angle" on the side triangles. The little notch is important for aligning the side triangles to the center triangle during construction.

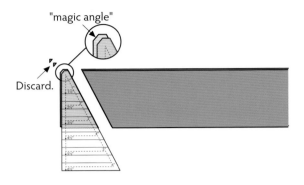

3 Rotate the Recs Tool so that the tip is aligned with the bottom edge of the strip and the marked line that corresponds to the unfinished size of your triangle unit is aligned with the top of the strip. The angled edge of the tool should be aligned with the angle edge of the strip. Cut along the straight edge of the Recs Tool to release the next pair of side triangles.

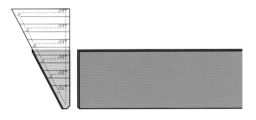

4 Repeat the process across the width of the strip. If needed, make straightening cuts as you go.

A Different Angle

Aligning the center and side triangles is a little different when using Bloc Loc rulers. Whereas the Tri-Recs templates have an alignment notch (or "magic angle") cut from the side triangle, the Bloc Loc alignment notch is cut from the center triangle. The narrow end of the right-side triangle is still aligned with the bottom-right corner of the center triangle, but the flat top of the side triangle will be flush with the angled notch of the center triangle.

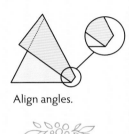

Align angles.

Stitching the Triangles

I'm a batch sewist, meaning I prefer to complete one step for all my blocks at once instead of sewing one complete block at a time. If you're making a quilt in this book, you're not likely to be making just one triangle unit at a time—you'll probably want to make all of the units at once. In this section, I'll include some of my tips for batch sewing and chain piecing.

1 To make chain piecing more efficient, sort the side triangles into a left-side pile and a right-side pile. Position the pile of right-side triangles wrong side up and with the narrow end pointing toward you.

2 Place a right-side triangle on a center triangle, right sides together, and align with the right edge of the center triangle. The narrow end of the side triangle will be at the bottom edge of the center triangle, and the little magic angle notch will align

precisely with the bottom-right corner of the center triangle. (You'll see the tip of the center triangle corner peek out—it's supposed to do that!)

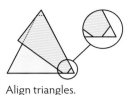

Align triangles.

3 Sew the triangles together using a *scant* ¼" seam allowance and continue sewing just a little beyond the edge of the fabric at the end of the seam. Do not clip the thread.

4 Without lifting the presser foot or cutting the thread, position a right-side triangle on top of another center triangle, right sides together and aligned as before. Stitch a *scant* ¼" seam allowance. The two triangle units will be connected by a little chain of thread, hence the term "chain piecing." Continue in this manner until you have sewn a right-side triangle to all of the center triangles. Snip the connecting thread between each unit before the next step.

5 With the side triangle on top and using lots of steam, quickly press the unopened seam to set the stitches. Then open the triangles and press the seam allowances toward the side triangle.

Make It Work

We're working with bias-cut edges here. It doesn't take much to warp those edges, especially when you're chain piecing and batch-pressing 50–100 triangles in a row. Here's how to work with those slightly warped triangles.

If you line up the edge of the side triangle precisely with the edge of the center triangle and the little tails of the right and left side triangles don't overlap, your center triangle is probably a little warped. If you stitch the side triangle with the edge lined up with the center triangle edge and press the side triangle open, you won't have a ¼" seam allowance at the top of the unit and you'll lose the point of your center triangle.

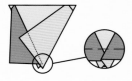

Instead of perfectly aligning the side edges of the side triangle and the center triangle, make sure the tails of the side triangles overlap exactly on top of each other. You may see a little bit of the center triangle peeking out from under the side triangle—that's OK. Making sure the tails are overlapped is more important so that you have full ¼" seam allowance beyond the tip of the center triangle.

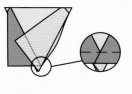

6 Position a center unit from step 5 so the bottom edge is at the top. Place the side triangles next to the center units, *wrong side up* and with the narrow tip pointing toward the top. Place a side triangle on top of the center triangle, right sides together and raw edges aligned. Align the magic angle notch with the upper-right corner of the center triangle. Stitch along the edge of the side triangle using a *scant* ¼" seam allowance.

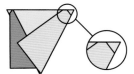

Align triangles.

7 Repeat the chain-piecing and pressing process as before. Trim your triangle units to the size indicated in the pattern.

You've Got a Point!

Paper-Foundation Piecing

Corn Maze (page 28) and Ribbon Rosettes (page 72) feature triangle-in-a-square units that are designed for paper-foundation piecing. It might be surprising to see paper-pieced units combined with traditionally pieced blocks in one full-size quilt pattern, but using this technique allowed me to create the designs I wanted without requiring additional specialty rulers.

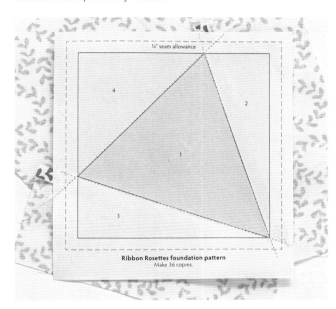

Stitch the block on the paper side, with the fabrics extending beyond the edges of the paper.

Trim on the outer lines of the paper to complete the block.

If you're completely new to the technique, Martingale has an excellent primer on paper-foundation piecing, which you can find at ShopMartingale.com/HowtoQuilt. The free tutorial will give you a great *foundation* (pardon the pun) for understanding the principles of paper piecing.

What follows here is a very specific tutorial on making the paper-pieced units in my quilts. The paper-pieced unit is the same in both quilts, and therefore the construction is also the same; the only difference is the finished size of the units in each pattern. Again, when I'm sewing, I like to complete one step for every block at once, so I've written the fabric cutting instructions and tutorial with the goal of making construction as close to batch-sewing as possible. That way you can more quickly knock out all the blocks in one sitting (if that's your jam).

You'll need one paper-foundation pattern for each unit within a block. Use lightweight paper that's easy to tear away, such as newsprint or Papers for Foundation Piecing by Martingale, which is made for running through your printer or copier.

There are four components to the paper-pieced units: a center triangle, two side triangles, and a tail triangle. The cutting instructions list the square size required for the center triangles. The squares are the same size as the unfinished unit. For the side triangles, you'll cut two identically sized rectangles, so you don't have to worry about keeping track of which piece is used for the left or right triangles. Finally, you'll cut rectangles in a different size for the tail triangle.

1 Copy the foundation pattern for the quilt you're making. Use a rotary cutter and ruler to trim the paper pattern just outside the dashed seam-allowance line. I use an older, dull blade for cutting paper.

2 Arrange the foundation with the blank (unprinted) side facing upward. Place a fabric square for area 1 right side up on the paper foundation, making sure the square is centered on the pattern. Secure with a pin.

3 Place one side triangle rectangle (piece 2) right side up on your sewing machine and align it with the ¼" guideline on the machine's sole plate (or Diagonal Seam Tape; see "Easy Guide Line" at right).

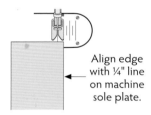

Align edge with ¼" line on machine sole plate.

4 Shorten the stitch length on your machine. Place the paper side up (fabric side down) on top of the rectangle, aligning the line between areas 1 and 2 with your sewing-machine needle. Stitch on the line, backstitching at the beginning and end of the line.

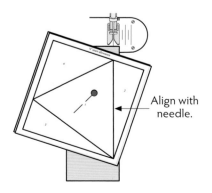

Align with needle.

Easy Guide Line

I've always wished for a better way to line up my fabric pieces when foundation-paper piecing, instead of holding the template and fabrics up to the light and hoping that I've correctly eyeballed that ¼" seam allowance all around. As I was working on the paper-pieced units for this book, I had a revelation. I could use the guide lines of the Diagonal Seam Tape adhered to the front plate on my sewing machine to easily and confidently line up my fabric pieces for paper piecing.

Diagonal Seam Tape was developed by Allison Harris of Cluck Cluck Sew as a way to sew diagonal seams (for half-square-triangle units and flying geese, for example) without having to mark a guideline from corner to corner on your fabric. But the perfect ¼" guidelines printed on the washi tape work just as well for eliminating the guesswork of lining up the fabric pieces during the paper-piecing process.

5 Fold back the paper and trim the excess fabric, leaving a ¼" seam allowance. Press piece 2 open using a hot, dry iron (steam will wrinkle the paper). Remove the pin.

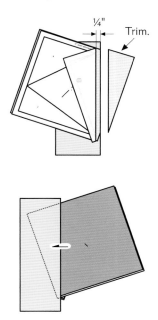

6 Repeat step 3–5 using the side-triangle rectangle for piece 3.

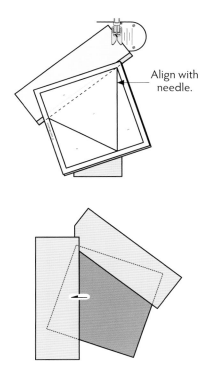

7 Repeat the steps to add the tail rectangle for piece 4.

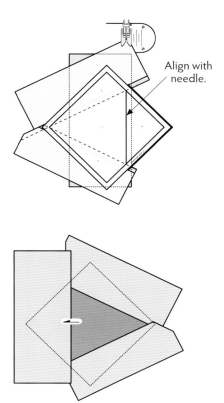

8 Use a rotary cutter and ruler to trim the completed unit along the dashed lines. Remove the paper foundations to make sewing the units into blocks easier.

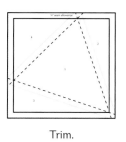

Trim.

Backgammon

Backgammon is a simple but striking quilt in a Goldilocks-worthy size—not too big, not too small, but just right for draping over a sofa or cuddling under during movie night. It's also a perfect introduction to triangle-in-a-square blocks, as the blocks are a great size for beginners. I used Civil War reproduction fabrics, but wouldn't this make a great high school or college graduation gift in the grad's school colors?

Finished quilt: 56½" × 66½"
Finished block: 6" × 6"

Materials

Yardage is based on 42"-wide fabric. Fat eighths measure 9" × 21". Fabric requirements and cutting instructions are for a Tri-Recs Tool Set. If you're using a Bloc Loc Ruler Set, increase the amount of fabric for the triangle units by about 25% (19 fat eighths of prints and 2⅞ yards of eggshell solid).

- 15 fat eighths of assorted prints for triangle units
- 2⅝ yards of eggshell solid for triangle units and sashing
- ¾ yard of tan print for border
- ½ yard of blue print for binding
- 3½ yards of fabric for backing
- 63" × 73" piece of batting
- Tri-Recs Tool set *OR* 6" × 6" Bloc Loc Triangle in a Square Ruler Set *OR* template plastic

Make It Scrappy

You'll make 60 triangle-in-a-square blocks for this quilt. You can comfortably cut four center triangles from one fat eighth, so you'll need 15 fat eighths. For a scrappier look, use more fat eighths—I used 30 for this quilt.

Cutting

All measurements include ¼" seam allowances. If you're not using Tri-Recs Tools or a Bloc Loc Triangle in a Square Ruler Set, trace the patterns for the center and side triangles on page 79 onto template plastic and cut them out. Refer to "Cutting the Triangles" on page 9 for detailed instructions as needed.

From *each* of the assorted prints, cut:
1 strip, 6½" × 21"; using a Tri-Recs Tool or center triangle template, cut the strips into 4 center triangles (60 total)

Continued on page 18

Assembling the Quilt Top

1 Join 10 blocks as shown to make a column. Make six columns measuring 6½" × 60½", including seam allowances.

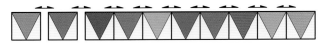

Make 6 columns,
6½" × 60½".

2 Join the eggshell 2½"-wide strips end to end. From the pieced strip, cut three 60½"-long sashing strips.

3 Sew an eggshell sashing strip between two block columns, making sure the center triangles are pointing toward the sashing strip. Make three backgammon columns measuring 14½" × 60½", including seam allowances.

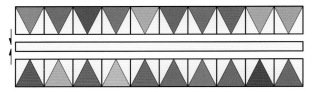

Make 3 columns,
14½" × 60½".

Continued from page 17

From the eggshell solid, cut:

8 strips, 6½" × 42"; keeping strips folded in half with selvedges together, use a Tri-Recs Tool or side triangle template to cut the strips into 60 pairs of side triangles

5 strips, 2½" × 42"

4 strips, 4½" × 42"

From the tan print, cut:

7 strips, 3½" × 42"

From the blue print, cut *on the bias*:

2½"-wide strips to total 270"

Making the Blocks

Press seam allowances in the directions indicated by the arrows.

Referring to "Making Triangle-in-a-Square Units" on page 6, use the print center triangles and eggshell side triangles to make a total of 60 blocks. Trim the blocks to 6½" square, including seam allowances.

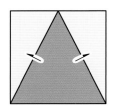

Make 60 blocks,
6½" × 6½".

Pin Point

Even if you're not generally a pinner, in this case, it's very helpful to pin the pieced strips to the sashing strip so you can keep the triangle points matched up across from one another as you sew the rows together.

Pieced by Anna Dineen and quilted by Amanda Birdwell

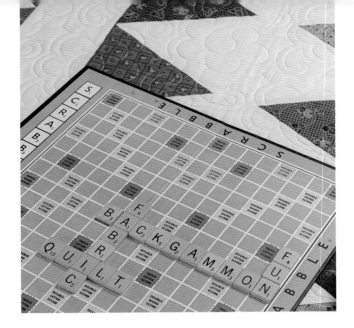

5 Join the tan 3½"-wide strips end to end. From the pieced strip, cut two 60½"-long strips and sew them to the left and right sides of the quilt. Cut two 56½"-long strips and sew them to the top and bottom edges. The quilt top should measure 56½" × 66½".

Finishing the Quilt

For more details on any of the finishing steps, go to ShopMartingale.com/HowtoQuilt to download free illustrated information.

1 Layer the quilt top, batting, and backing; baste the layers together.

2 Quilt by hand or machine. The quilt shown is machine quilted with an allover flower design.

3 Trim the excess batting and backing. Use the blue 2½"-wide bias strips to make double-fold binding and attach the binding to the quilt.

4 Join the eggshell 4½"-wide strips end to end. From the pieced strip, cut two 60½"-long sashing strips. Referring to the quilt assembly diagram below, join the backgammon columns from step 3 and the 4½"-wide sashing strips. The quilt-top center should measure 50½" × 60½", including seam allowances.

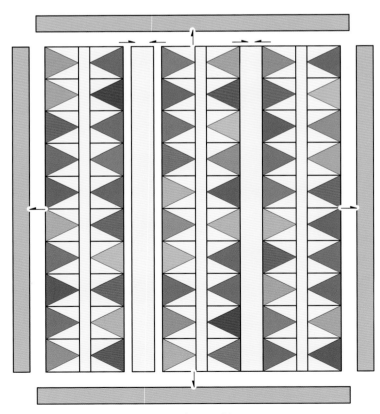

Quilt assembly

Smoke Rings

Sometimes I'll see a fabric collection and design a quilt specifically for it. That was the case with Smoke Rings—the beautiful shades of black and gray in the fabric collection used here seemed ready-made for a design that featured an ombré effect. But I could also see this pattern used to make a cheerful table topper featuring rainbow rings or as a scrappy, one-color showcase for your favorite color.

Finished quilt: 42½" × 42½"
Finished block: 12" × 12"

Materials

Yardage is based on 42"-wide fabric. Fat eighths measure 9" × 21". Fabric requirements and cutting instructions are for a Tri-Recs Tool set. If you're using a Bloc Loc Ruler Set, increase the amount of fabric for the triangle units (4 fat quarters of rust prints instead of fat eighths and 2 yards of eggshell).

- 1⅝ yards of eggshell solid for blocks
- 4 fat eighths of assorted rust prints for blocks
- 6 fat eighths of assorted black prints for blocks
- 2 fat eighths of assorted light gray prints for blocks
- 2 fat eighths of assorted slate prints for blocks
- 2 fat eighths of assorted charcoal prints for blocks
- ½ yard of cream print for border
- ⅜ yard of rust print for binding
- 2¾ yards of fabric for backing
- 49" × 49" piece of batting
- Tri-Recs Tool set or 2" × 2" Bloc Loc Triangle in a Square Ruler Set OR template plastic

Cutting

All measurements include ¼" seam allowances. If you're not using Tri-Recs Tools or a Bloc Loc Triangle in a Square Ruler Set, trace the patterns for the center and side triangles on page 79 onto template plastic and cut them out. Refer to "Cutting the Triangles" on page 9 for detailed instructions as needed.

From the eggshell solid, cut:

4 strips, 4½" × 42"; crosscut into 64 strips, 1⅞" × 4½"

1 strip, 3⅛" × 42"; crosscut into 16 pieces, 1⅞" × 3⅛"

7 strips, 2½" × 42"; keeping the strips folded in half with selvedge edges together, use a Recs Tool or side triangle template to cut the strips into 100 pairs of side triangles

4 strips, 1⅞" × 42"; crosscut into 80 squares, 1⅞" × 1⅞"

4 strips, 1½" × 42"; crosscut into:
• 2 strips, 1½" × 38½"
• 2 strips, 1½" × 36½"

From *each of 3* rust fat eighths, cut:

3 strips, 2½" × 21"; use a Tri Tool or center triangle template to cut the strips into 24 center triangles (72 total)

From the remaining rust fat eighth, cut:

3 strips, 2½" × 21"; use a Tri Tool or center triangle template to cut the strips into 28 center triangles

From *each* black fat eighth, cut:

2 strips, 4½" × 9"; crosscut into 6 strips, 1⅞" × 4½" (36 total; 4 will be extra)

From *each of 4* remaining black fat eighths, cut:

4 squares, 1⅞" × 1⅞" (16 total)

From *1* light gray fat eighth, cut:

1 strip, 1⅞" × 9"; crosscut into 4 squares, 1⅞" × 1⅞"

1 strip, 3⅛" × 9"; crosscut into 4 pieces, 1⅞" × 3⅛"

From the remaining light gray fat eighth, cut:

2 strips, 1⅞" × 9"; crosscut into 8 squares, 1⅞" × 1⅞"

From *1* slate fat eighth, cut:

1 strip, 1⅞" × 9"; crosscut into 4 squares, 1⅞" × 1⅞"

1 strip, 3⅛" × 9"; crosscut into 4 pieces, 1⅞" × 3⅛"

From the remaining slate fat eighth, cut:

2 strips, 1⅞" × 9"; crosscut into 8 squares, 1⅞" × 1⅞"

1 strip, 4½" × 9"; crosscut into 4 strips, 1⅞" × 4½"

From *1* charcoal fat eighth, cut:

2 strips, 1⅞" × 9"; crosscut into 8 squares, 1⅞" × 1⅞"

2 strips, 3⅛" × 9"; crosscut into 8 pieces, 1⅞" × 3⅛"

From the remaining charcoal fat eighth, cut:

1 strip, 4½" × 9"; crosscut into 4 strips, 1⅞" × 4½"

From the cream print, cut:

5 strips, 2½" × 42"

From the rust print, cut *on the bias*:

2½"-wide strips to total 185"

Making the Units

Press seam allowances in the directions indicated by the arrows.

1 Referring to "Making Triangle-in-a-Square Units" on page 6, use the rust center triangles and eggshell side triangles to make 25 sets of four matching triangle units (100 total). Trim each unit to 2½" square, including seam allowances.

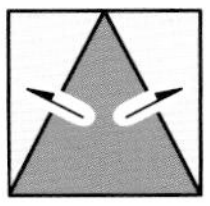

Make 25 sets of 4 matching units, 2½" × 2½".

2 Lay out four matching triangle units in two rows as shown. Sew the units into rows and then join the rows to make a pinwheel unit. Make 25 units measuring 4½" square, including seam allowances.

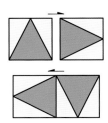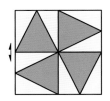

Make 25 Pinwheel units, 4½" × 4½".

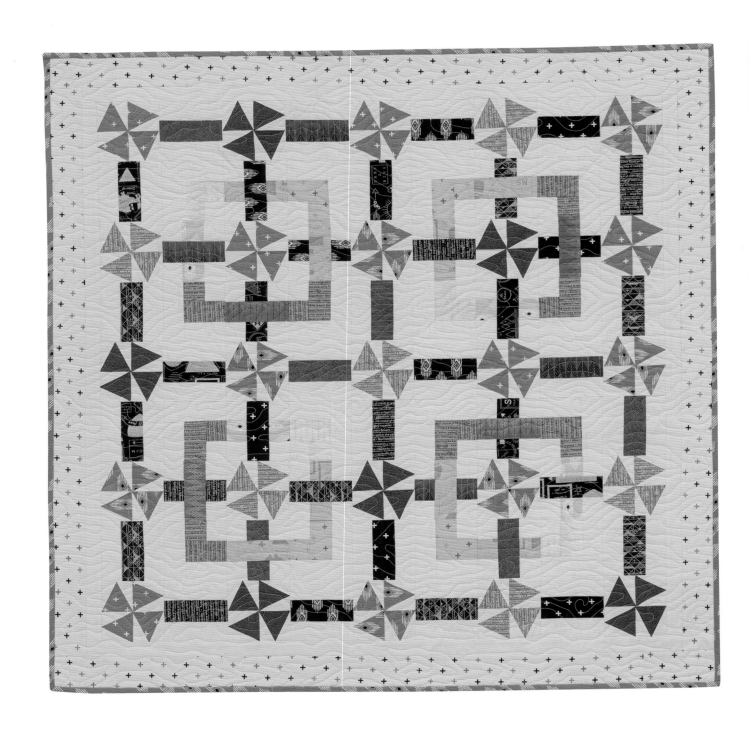

Pieced by Anna Dineen and quilted by Amanda Birdwell

You've Got a Point!

3 Join two eggshell 1⅞" × 4½" strips and one black strip to make a dash unit. Make 24 units and trim them to 4½" square, including seam allowances, keeping the black strip centered.

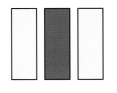

Make 24 Dash units,
4½" × 4½".

4 Join a light gray and an eggshell 1⅞" square to make a two-square unit. Join a light gray and an eggshell 1⅞" × 3⅛" piece. Sew the unit to the left side of the two-square unit. The light gray should be the same throughout. Make four light gray units and trim either side so the unit measures 3⅛" × 4½", including seam allowances.

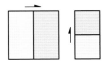

Make 4 units,
3⅛" × 4½".

5 Sew an eggshell 1⅞" × 4½" strip to the top of a unit from step 4 to make a corner unit. Make four light gray corner units that measure 4½" square, including seam allowances.

Make 4 light gray corner units,
4½" × 4½".

6 Repeat steps 4 and 5 to make four slate and eight charcoal corner units measuring 4½" square, including seam allowances.

Make 4 slate corner units,   Make 8 charcoal corner units,
4½" × 4½".   4½" × 4½".

7 Join two eggshell 1⅞" squares and one light gray square. Make two matching units. Sew the units to opposite sides of a black 1⅞" × 4½" rectangle to make a cross A unit. Make four light gray units measuring 4½" square, including seam allowances. Repeat to make four slate cross A units.

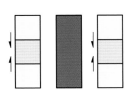 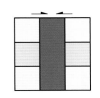

Make 4 light gray A units,
4½" × 4½".

Make 4 slate A units,
4½" × 4½".

Keep it Simple

Don't be intimidated by all the pieces in these blocks! To make construction simpler, I've written the instructions so that matching prints are used within each unit. For example, you'll use one light gray print for all light gray corner units and a second light gray print for all the cross A units.

8 Join two eggshell 1⅞" squares and one black square. Make two matching units. Sew the unit to opposite sides of a slate 1⅞" × 4½" strip to make a cross B unit. Make four slate units measuring 4½" square, including seam allowances. Repeat to make four charcoal cross B units.

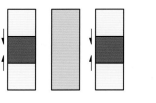

Make 4 slate B units,
4½" × 4½".

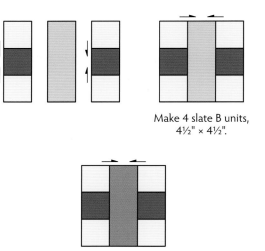

Make 4 charcoal B units,
4½" × 4½".

Making the Blocks

Referring to the diagram, lay out a light gray corner unit, a slate cross A unit, and a slate corner unit for the top row. Lay out one light gray cross A unit, one pinwheel unit, and one slate cross B unit for the center row. Lay out two charcoal corner units and

one charcoal cross B units for the bottom row. Sew the units into rows and then join the rows. Make four blocks measuring 12½" square, including seam allowances.

Make 4 blocks,
12½" × 12½".

Assembling the Quilt Top

1 Join one pinwheel unit and two dash units to make a sashing unit. Make six units measuring 4½" × 12½", including seam allowances.

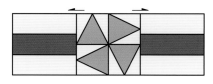

Make 6 sashing units,
4½" × 12½".

You've Got a Point!

2 Join five pinwheel units and four dash units, alternating their positions as shown to make a pinwheel row. Make three rows measuring 4½" × 36½", including seam allowances.

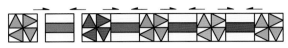

Make 3 pinwheel rows,
4½" × 36½".

3 Join three sashing units and two blocks to make a block row. Make two block rows that measure 12½" × 36½".

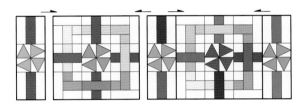

Make 2 block rows,
12½" × 36½".

4 Join the pinwheel rows and block rows as shown. The quilt-top center should measure 36½" square, including seam allowances.

Quilt assembly

5 Sew the eggshell 1½" × 36½" strips to the left and right sides of the quilt top. Sew the eggshell 1½" × 38½" strips to the top and bottom edges. Press all seam allowances toward the eggshell strips. The quilt top should measure 38½" square, including seam allowances.

6 Join the cream print 2½"-wide strips end to end. From the pieced strip, cut two 38½"-long strips and sew them to the left and right sides of the quilt top. Cut two 42½"-long strips and sew them to the top and bottom edges. Press all seam allowances toward the outer border. The quilt top should measure 42½" square.

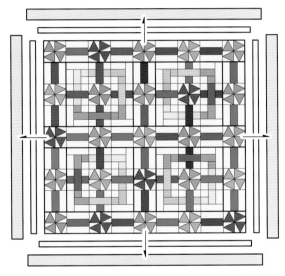

Adding the borders

Finishing the Quilt

For more details on any of the finishing steps, go to ShopMartingale.com/HowtoQuilt to download free illustrated information.

1 Layer the quilt top, batting, and backing; baste the layers together.

2 Quilt by hand or machine. The quilt shown is machine quilted with an allover wood-grain design.

3 Trim the excess batting and backing. Use the rust 2½"-wide bias strips to make double-fold binding and attach the binding to the quilt.

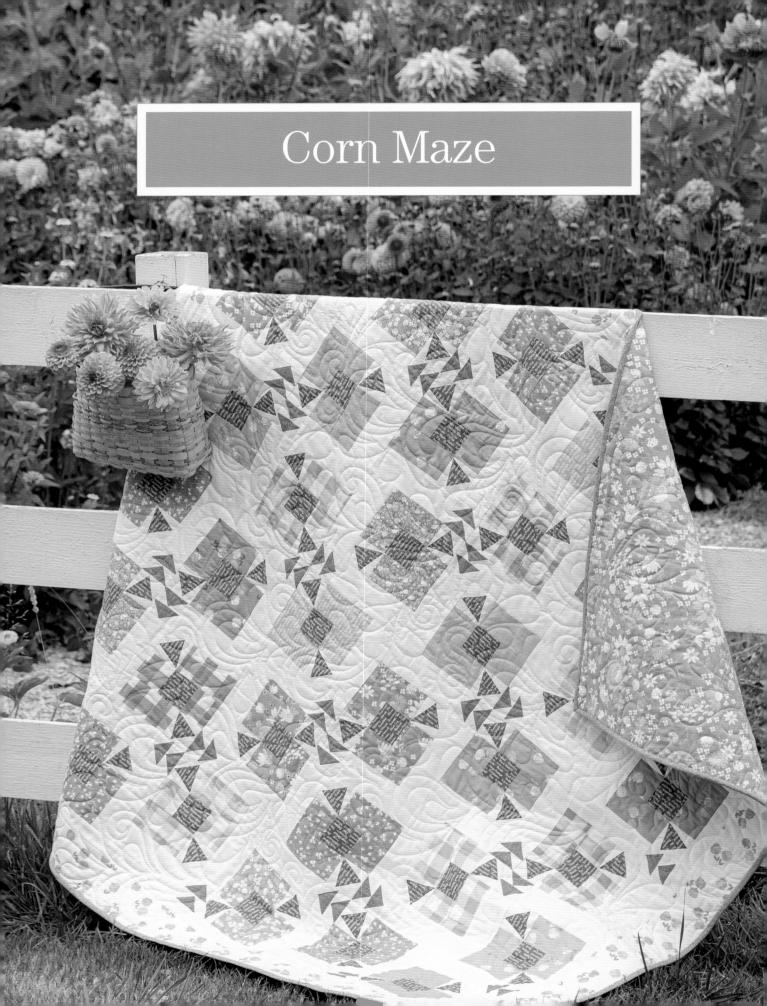

Corn Maze

I love how the flying-geese units in Corn Maze seem to make paths that crisscross the quilt, creating a secondary pattern and a sense of movement. Rather than toss in some low-volume or light prints for the blocks, I used all medium-value prints to keep the colors balanced across the quilt. A light-background floral for the border keeps the focus on the blocks instead of competing with the overall design.

Finished quilt: 56½" × 56½"
Finished block: 8" × 8"

Materials

Yardage is based on 42"-wide fabric.

- 2⅝ yards of ivory solid for blocks and inner border
- ⅝ yard of black A print for blocks
- ¼ yard of black B print for blocks
- 18 squares, 10" × 10", of assorted prints in orange, yellow, olive, and teal for blocks
- ⅔ yard of light floral for outer border
- ½ yard of teal print for binding
- 3½ yards of fabric for backing
- 63" × 63" piece of batting
- Paper for foundation piecing (see page 13)
- Bloc Loc 1" × 2" Flying Geese Ruler Set (optional)

Cutting

All measurements include ¼" seam allowances.

From the ivory solid, cut:

8 strips, 3¼" × 42"; crosscut into 144 pieces, 2" × 3¼"

4 strips, 3" × 42"; crosscut into 72 pieces, 2" × 3"

12 strips, 2½" × 42"; crosscut into 72 strips, 2½" × 6½"

11 strips, 1½" × 42"; crosscut *6 of the strips* into 144 squares, 1½" × 1½"*

From the black A print, cut:

7 strips, 2½" × 42"; crosscut into 108 squares, 2½" × 2½"

From the black B print, cut:

3 strips, 2½" × 42"; crosscut into 72 pieces, 1½" × 2½"*

*If you're using a Bloc Loc 1" × 2" Flying Geese Ruler Set, you'll need to make the flying-geese units oversized. Instead of cutting ivory 1½" squares and black B 1½" × 2½" pieces, cut ivory 1¾" squares and black B 1¾" × 2¾" pieces. Following the instructions in step 3 on page 30, make 72 flying-geese units and then trim the units to measure 1½" × 2½", including seam allowances. To use the Bloc Loc method, you'll need 2⅔ yards of ivory and ⅓ yard of black.

Continued on page 30

Continued from page 29

From *each* assorted print square, cut:

4 squares, 2½" × 2½" (72 total)

4 pieces, 2½" × 4½" (72 total)

From the light floral, cut:

6 strips, 3½" × 42"

From the teal print, cut on the *bias*:

2½"-wide strips to total 240"

Making the Blocks

Press seam allowances in the directions indicated by the arrows.

1 Make 72 copies of the foundation pattern on page 33.

2 Referring to "Paper-Foundation Piecing" on page 13, paper piece 72 triangle units as follows:

- Piece 1: black A 2½" square
- Pieces 2 and 3: ivory 2" × 3¼" pieces
- Piece 4: ivory 2" × 3" piece

Make 72 units,
2½" × 2½".

3 Draw a diagonal line from corner to corner on the wrong side of the ivory 1½" squares. Place a marked square on one end of a black B 1½" × 2½" piece, right sides together. Sew on the marked line. Trim the excess corner fabric ¼" from the stitched line. Place a marked square on the opposite end of the black piece. Sew and trim as before to make a flying-geese unit. Make 72 units measuring 1½" × 2½", including seam allowances.

Make 72 units,
1½" × 2½".

4 Join two flying-geese units as shown to make a double flying-geese unit. Sew the geese unit to one end of an ivory 2½" × 6½" piece. Make 36 units measuring 2½" × 8½", including seam allowances.

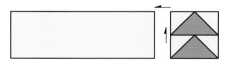

Make 36 side units,
2½" × 8½".

You've Got a Point!

Pieced by Anna Dineen and quilted by Carrie Straka

5 Lay out two triangle units, two matching print 2½" × 4½" pieces, two matching print 2½" squares, and one black A 2½" square in three rows. Sew all the pieces into rows and then join the rows. Make 36 units measuring 6½" square, including seam allowances.

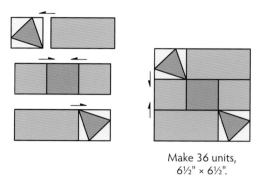

Make 36 units,
6½" × 6½".

6 Lay out one unit from step 4, one ivory 2½" × 6½" piece, and one unit from step 5 as shown. Join all the pieces to make a block. Make 36 blocks measuring 8½" square, including seam allowances.

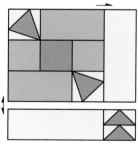

Make 36 blocks,
8½" × 8½".

Assembling the Quilt Top

1 Referring to the quilt assembly diagram, lay out the blocks in six rows of six blocks each, rotating the blocks in each row and from row to row as shown. Notice that the orientation of the rotated blocks is the same in every other row and that the black pieces form a diagonal grid. Sew the blocks into rows and then join the rows. The quilt-top center should measure 48½" square, including seam allowances.

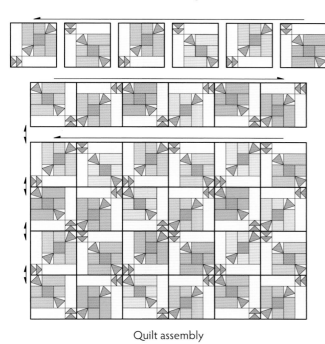

Quilt assembly

2 Join the ivory 1½"-wide strips end to end. From the pieced strip, cut two 48½"-long strips and sew them to the left and right sides of the quilt top. Cut two 50½"-long strips and sew them to the top and bottom edges. Press all seam allowances toward the ivory strips. The quilt top should measure 50½" square, including seam allowances.

3 Join the light floral 3½"-wide strips end to end. From the pieced strip, cut two 50½"-long strips and sew them to the left and right sides of the quilt top. Cut two 56½"-long strips and sew them to the top and bottom edges. Press all seam allowances toward the outer border. The quilt top should measure 56½" square.

Finishing the Quilt

For more details on any of the finishing steps, go to ShopMartingale.com/HowtoQuilt to download free illustrated information.

1 Layer the quilt top, batting, and backing; baste the layers together.

2 Quilt by hand or machine. The quilt shown is machine quilted with an allover meandering feather design.

3 Trim the excess batting and backing. Use the teal print 2½"-wide bias strips to make double-fold binding and attach the binding to the quilt.

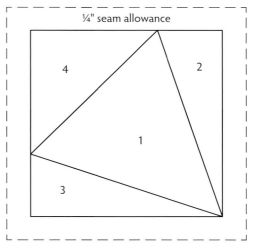

Corn Maze foundation pattern
Make 72 copies.

Cut Glass

The secondary patterns here are really the stars of the show. The solid white center triangles join together to form bold diamonds, while the subtle ombré shading in the quarter-log-cabin units gives the appearance of curves. Custom quilting, rather than an edge-to-edge pantograph, helps bring those secondary patterns into focus. The result is a quilt that reminds me of my prized crystal and cut-glass stemware!

Finished quilt: 72½" × 72½"
Finished block: 12" × 12"

Materials

Yardage is based on 42"-wide fabric. Fabric requirements and cutting instructions are for a Tri-Recs Tool set. If you're using a Bloc Loc Ruler Set, increase the amount of fabric for the triangle units by about 25% (⅝ yard each of the 5 red prints and 2 yards of ivory solid). Label each of your light and green prints with letters to make cutting and piecing easier.

♦ ⅛ yard *each* of light A and light B prints for blocks

♦ ⅓ yard *each* of light green A and dark green A prints for blocks

♦ ½ yard *each* of light green B and dark green B prints for blocks

♦ ⅝ yard *each* of light green C and dark green C prints for blocks

♦ ½ yard *each* of 5 assorted red prints for blocks

♦ 1⅔ yards of ivory solid for blocks and inner border

♦ 1⅛ yards of gray floral for outer border

♦ ⅝ yard of red print for binding

♦ 6¾ yards of fabric for backing

♦ 81" × 81" piece of batting

♦ Tri-Recs Tool set *OR* 4" × 4" Bloc Loc Triangle in a Square Ruler Set *OR* template plastic

Cutting

All measurements include ¼" seam allowances. If you're not using Tri-Recs Tools or a Bloc Loc Triangle in a Square Ruler set, trace the patterns for the center and side triangles on page 79 onto template plastic and cut them out. Refer to "Cutting the Triangles" on page 9 for detailed instructions as needed.

From the light A print, cut:
2 strips, 1½" × 42"; crosscut into 52 squares, 1½" × 1½"

From the light green A print, cut:
2 strips, 1½" × 42"; crosscut into 52 squares, 1½" × 1½"
2 strips, 2½" × 42"; crosscut into 52 pieces, 1½" × 2½"

From the light green B print, cut:
2 strips, 2½" × 42"; crosscut into 52 pieces, 1½" × 2½"
2 strips, 3½" × 42"; crosscut into 52 pieces, 1½" × 3½"

Continued on page 36

Continued from page 35

From the light green C print, cut:

2 strips, 3½" × 42"; crosscut into 52 pieces,
1½" × 3½"

2 strips, 4½" × 42"; crosscut into 52 pieces,
1½" × 4½"

From the light B print, cut:

2 strips, 1½" × 42"; crosscut into 48 squares,
1½" × 1½"

From the dark green A print, cut:

2 strips, 1½" × 42"; crosscut into 48 squares,
1½" × 1½"

2 strips, 2½" × 42"; crosscut into 48 pieces,
1½" × 2½"

From the dark green B print, cut:

2 strips, 2½" × 42"; crosscut into 48 pieces,
1½" × 2½"

2 strips, 3½" × 42"; crosscut into 48 pieces,
1½" × 3½"

From the dark green C print, cut:

2 strips, 3½" × 42"; crosscut into 48 pieces,
1½" × 3½"

2 strips, 4½" × 42"; crosscut into 48 pieces,
1½" × 4½"

From *each* of the assorted red prints, cut:

2 strips, 4½" × 42"; keeping the strips folded in half,
selvedge edges together, use a Recs Tool or side
triangle template to cut the strips into 20 pairs of
side triangles (100 pairs total)

1 strip, 4½" × 42"; crosscut into 5 squares,
4½" × 4½" (25 total)

From the ivory solid, cut:

8 strips, 4½" × 42"; use a Tri Tool or center
triangle template to cut the strips into 100
center triangles

7 strips, 2½" × 42"

From the gray floral, cut:

8 strips, 4½" × 42"

From the red print for binding, cut *on the bias*:

2½"-wide strips to total 310"

Making the Quarter-Log-Cabin Units

The fabric placement in each quarter-log-cabin unit is designed to gradually darken from the square outward to create an ombré effect. The lightest prints in the corner of each unit meet to give the appearance of rings in the finished quilt. Press seam allowances in the directions indicated by the arrows.

1 Sew a light A square to the right side of a light green A square. Sew a light green A 1½" × 2½" piece to the bottom of the unit. Make 52 units measuring 2½" square, including seam allowances.

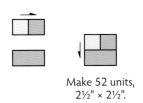

Make 52 units,
2½" × 2½".

2 Sew a light green B 1½" × 2½" piece to the right side of the unit. Sew a light green B 1½" × 3½" piece to the bottom of the unit. Make 52 units measuring 3½" square, including seam allowances.

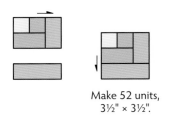

Make 52 units,
3½" × 3½".

3 Sew a light green C 1½" × 3½" piece to the right side and a light green C 1½" × 4½" piece to the bottom of the unit to make a quarter-log-cabin unit. Make 52 units measuring 4½" square, including seam allowances.

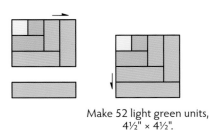

Make 52 light green units,
4½" × 4½".

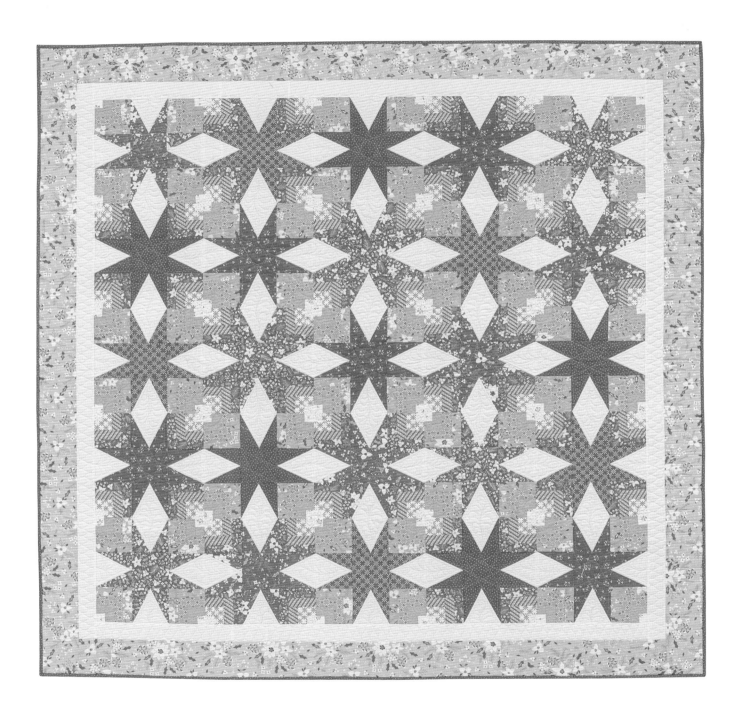

Pieced by Anna Dineen and quilted by Maggi Honeyman

Assembling the Blocks

1 Referring to "Making Triangle-in-a-Square Units" on page 6, use the ivory center triangles and two red side triangles to make 25 sets of four matching triangle units (100 total). Trim each unit to 4½" square, including seam allowances.

Make 25 sets of 4 matching units, 4½" × 4½".

2 Lay out four matching quarter-log-cabin units, four matching triangle units from step 1, and one matching red 4½" square in three rows. Sew the units into rows and then join the rows to make a block. Make 13 light green and 12 dark green blocks measuring 12½" square, including seam allowances.

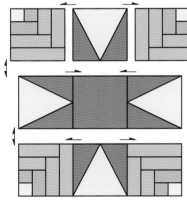

Make 13 light green blocks, 12½" × 12½".

4 Repeat steps 1–3 using the light B squares and the dark green A–C pieces to make 48 dark green units measuring 4½" square, including seam allowances.

Make 48 dark green units, 4½" × 4½".

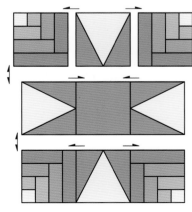

Make 12 dark green blocks, 12½" × 12½".

Assembling the Quilt Top

1 Referring to the quilt assembly diagram below, lay out the light green and dark green blocks in five rows of five blocks each, alternating the light and dark blocks in each row and from row to row. Sew the blocks into rows and then join the rows. The quilt-top center should measure 60½" square, including seam allowances.

2 Join the ivory 2½"-wide strips end to end. From the pieced strip, cut two 60½"-long strips and sew them to the left and right sides of your quilt top. Cut two 64½"-long strips and sew them to the top and bottom edges. Press all seam allowances toward the ivory strips. The quilt top should measure 64½" square, including seam allowances.

3 Join the gray 4½"-wide strips end to end. From the pieced strip, cut two 64½"-long strips and sew them to the left and right sides of your quilt top. Cut two 72½"-long strips and sew them to the top and bottom edges. Press all seam allowances toward the outer border. The quilt top should measure 72½" square.

Finishing the Quilt

For more details on any of the finishing steps, go to ShopMartingale.com/HowtoQuilt to download free illustrated information.

1 Layer the quilt top, batting, and backing; baste the layers together.

2 Quilt by hand or machine. The quilt shown is machine quilted with a custom design that includes feather, star, and figure-eight motifs.

3 Trim the excess batting and backing. Use the red 2½"-wide bias strips to make double-fold binding and attach the binding to the quilt.

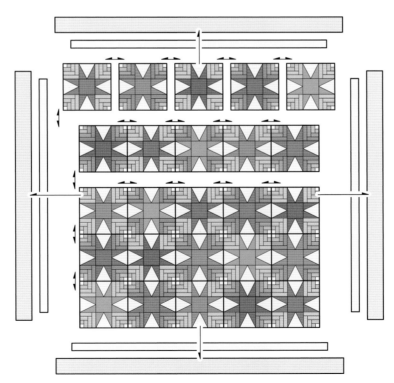

Quilt assembly

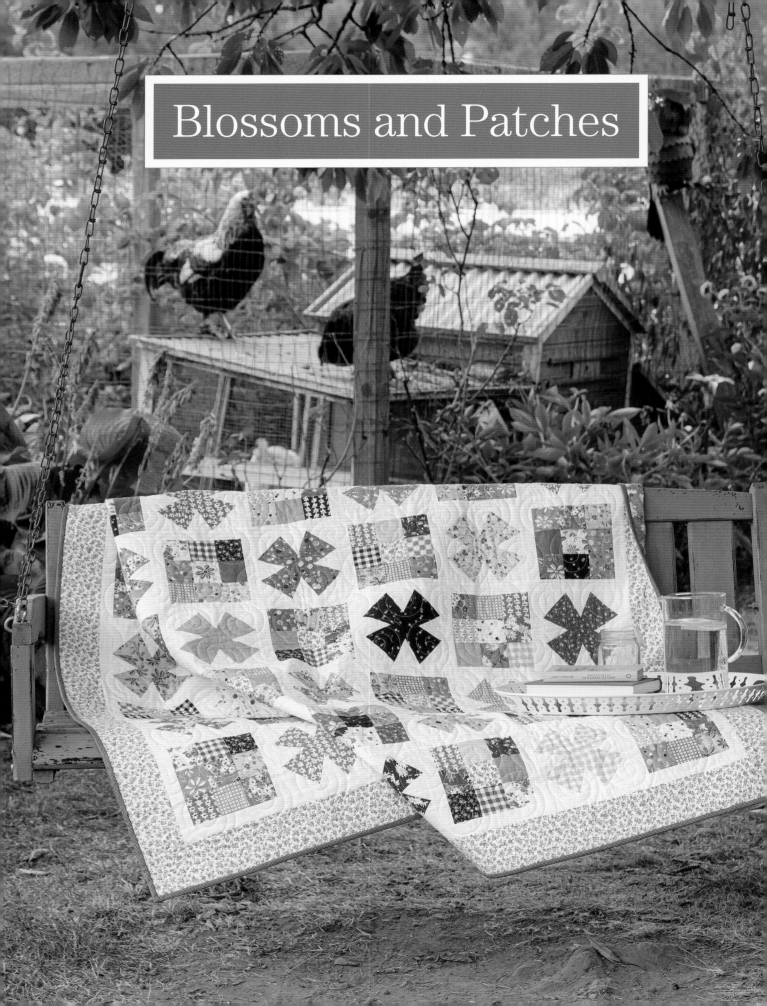

Blossoms and Patches

If there ever was a time to dig into your scrap bins, this is it! *Blossoms and Patches* is a sweet lap-sized quilt bursting with classic patchwork charm, especially when made with 1930s reproduction fabrics, as I did here. Though the pattern is written for fat eighths, it would be easy to adapt it to accommodate other precuts or scraps—for example, leftover Jelly Roll strips would be perfect for making the Nine Patch blocks.

Finished quilt: 56½" × 56½"
Finished block: 6" × 6"

Materials

Yardage is based on 42"-wide fabric. Fat eighths measure 9" × 21". Fabric requirements and cutting instructions are for a Tri-Recs Tool set. If you're using a Bloc Loc Ruler Set, increase the amount of ivory solid to 1¾ yards.

- 36 fat eighths in assorted prints for blocks
- 1⅝ yards of ivory solid for blocks and sashing
- ⅔ yard of orange floral for outer border
- ½ yard of blue print for binding
- 3½ yards of fabric for backing
- 63" × 63" piece of batting
- Tri-Recs Tool set *OR* 2" × 2" Bloc Loc Triangle in a Square Ruler Set *OR* template plastic

Cutting

All measurements include ¼" seam allowances. If you're not using Tri-Recs Tools or a Bloc Loc Triangle in a Square Ruler Set, trace the patterns for the center and side triangles on page 79 onto template plastic and cut them out. Refer to "Cutting the Triangles" on page 9 for detailed instructions as needed.

From *each* of 36 assorted prints, cut:
1 strip, 2½" × 18" (36 total)

From the remainder of *each* of 24 assorted prints, cut:
1 strip, 2½" × 18"; fold the strip in half crosswise, right sides together, and use a Tri-Recs Tool or side triangle template to cut the strip into 4 matching pairs of side triangles (96 pairs total)

2 squares, 3" × 3"; cut the squares in half diagonally to yield 4 triangles (96 total)

1 square, 2½" × 2½" (24 total)

Continued on page 42

Making the Nine Patch Blocks

Press seam allowances in the directions indicated by the arrows.

1 Join three different print strips to make a strip set. Make 12 strip sets measuring 6½" × 18", including seam allowances. Cut each of three strip sets into seven 2½" × 6½" segments (21 total). Cut each of the remaining nine strip sets into six 2½" × 6½" segments (54 total). You should have a total of 75 segments.

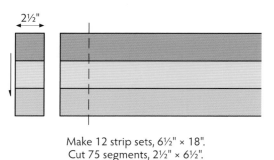

Make 12 strip sets, 6½" × 18".
Cut 75 segments, 2½" × 6½".

2 Join three different segments as shown to make a Nine Patch block. Make 25 blocks measuring 6½" square, including seam allowances.

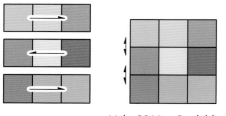

Make 25 Nine Patch blocks,
6½" × 6½".

Continued from page 41

From the ivory solid, cut:

4 strips, 2½" × 42"; use a Tri-Recs Tool or center triangle template to cut the strips into 96 center triangles

4 strips, 3" × 42"; crosscut into 48 squares, 3" × 3". Cut the squares in half diagonally to yield 96 triangles.

20 strips, 1½" × 42"; crosscut 7 *of the strips* into 42 strips, 1½" × 6½"

From the orange floral, cut:

6 strips, 3½" × 42"

From the blue print, cut *on the bias*:

2½"-wide strips to total 245"

Match the Seams

Because the strip set seam allowances are all pressed in one direction, rotating the segments to alternate the direction of the seam allowances will allow them to nest—and nested seams make for easier, more precise piecing.

You've Got a Point!

Pieced by Anna Dineen and quilted by Amanda Birdwell

Making the Blossom Blocks

1 Referring to "Making Triangle-in-a-Square Units" on page 6, use the ivory center triangles and print side triangles to make 24 sets of four matching triangle units (96 total). Trim the units to 2½" square, including seam allowances.

Make 24 sets of 4 matching units,
2½" × 2½".

2 Layer an ivory 3" triangle on top of a print 3" triangle, right sides together. Sew along the bias edge to make a half-square-triangle unit. Trim the unit to 2½" square, including seam allowances. Make 24 sets of four matching units (96 total).

Make 24 sets of
4 matching units.

3 Lay out four units from step 1, four units from step 2, and one print 2½" square in three rows as shown. The print should be the same throughout. Sew all the pieces into rows. Join the rows to make a Blossom block. Make 24 blocks measuring 6½" square, including seam allowances.

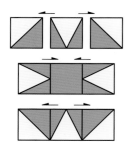 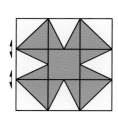

Make 24 Blossom blocks,
6½" × 6½".

Assembling the Quilt Top

1 Lay out four Nine Patch blocks, three Blossom blocks, and six ivory 1½" × 6½" strips, alternating their positions as shown. Join the blocks and strips to make row A. Make four rows measuring 6½" × 48½", including seam allowances.

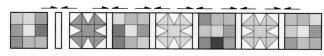

Make 4 of row A,
6½" × 48½".

2 Lay out four Blossom blocks, three Nine Patch blocks, and six ivory 1½" × 6½" strips, alternating their positions as shown. Join the blocks and strips to make row B. Make three rows measuring 6½" × 48½", including seam allowances.

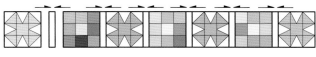

Make 3 of row B,
6½" × 48½".

3 Join eight ivory 1½"-wide strips end to end. From the pieced strip, cut six 48½"-long sashing strips.

4 Lay out the block rows and sashing strips, alternating their positions as shown in the quilt assembly diagram. Join the block rows and sashing strips to make the quilt-top center, which should measure 48½" square, including seam allowances.

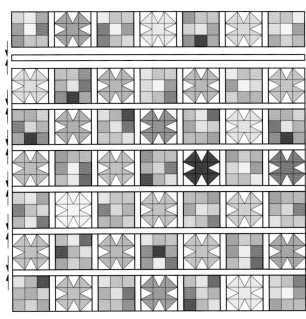

Quilt assembly

5 Join the remaining ivory 1½"-wide strips end to end. From the pieced strip, cut two 48½"-long strips and sew them to the left and right sides of the quilt top. Cut two 50½"-long strips and sew

them to the top and bottom edges. Press all seam allowances toward the ivory strips. The quilt top should measure 50½" square, including seam allowances.

6 Join the orange floral 3½"-wide strips end to end. From the pieced strip, cut two 50½"-long strips and sew them to the left and right sides of the quilt top. Cut two 56½"-long strips and sew them to the top and bottom edges. Press all seam allowances toward the outer border. The quilt top should measure 56½" square.

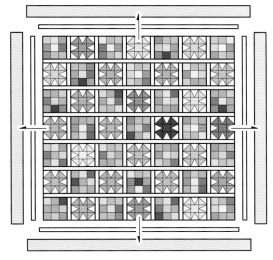

Adding the borders

Finishing the Quilt

For more details on any of the finishing steps, go to ShopMartingale.com/HowtoQuilt to download free illustrated information.

1 Layer the quilt top, batting, and backing; baste the layers together.

2 Quilt by hand or machine. The quilt shown is machine quilted with an allover swirl design.

3 Trim the excess batting and backing. Use the blue 2½"-wide bias strips to make double-fold binding and attach the binding to the quilt.

Thistledown

I collected traditional and Civil War reproduction prints from a variety of designers and manufacturers to create Thistledown, a quilt designed to capture the feel of Christmas past at a country manor. Along with the expected shades of Christmassy reds and greens, I included prints in bright poison green, blue-tinged mallard green, and soft rose to add interest—I love seeing the little pops of unexpected colors scattered throughout the quilt.

Finished quilt: 74½" × 74½"
Finished block: 10" × 10"

Materials

Yardage is based on 42"-wide fabric. Fat eighths measure 9" × 21". Fabric requirements and cutting instructions are for a Tri-Recs Tool set. If you're using a Bloc Loc Ruler Set, increase the amount of fabric for the triangle units (18 fat quarters of green prints instead of fat eighths and 3½ yards of eggshell solid).

♦ 3 yards of eggshell solid for block backgrounds

♦ 18 fat eighths of assorted green prints for blocks

♦ 18 fat eighths of assorted red prints for blocks

♦ 2⅛ yards of ivory print for sashing and borders

♦ ⅝ yard of red print for binding

♦ 7 yards of fabric for backing

♦ 83" × 83" piece of batting

♦ Tri-Recs Tool set *OR* 2" × 2" Bloc Loc Triangle in a Square Ruler set *OR* template plastic

Cutting

All measurements include ¼" seam allowances. If you're not using Tri-Recs Tools or a Bloc Loc Triangle in a Square Ruler Set, trace the patterns for the center and side triangles on page 79 onto template plastic and cut them out. Refer to "Cutting the Triangles" on page 6 for detailed instructions as needed

From the eggshell solid, cut:
31 strips, 2½" × 42"; crosscut into:

 288 center triangles using a Tri-Recs Tool or center triangle template

 288 squares, 2½" × 2½"

9 strips, 1⅞" × 42"; crosscut into 36 strips, 1⅞" × 9"

From *each* of the assorted green prints, cut on the *lengthwise* grain:
2 strips, 4" × 9"; crosscut into 4 squares, 4" × 4". Cut the squares in half diagonally to yield 8 triangles (144 total).

4 strips, 2½" × 9"; fold the strips in half crosswise, right sides together, and use a Tri-Recs Tool or side triangle template to cut the strips into 16 pairs of side triangles (288 pairs total)

Continued on page 48

Continued from page 47

From *each* of the assorted red prints, cut:

1 strip, 2" × 9" (18 total)

2 strips, 2"x 4¾" (36 total)

From the ivory print, cut:

27 strips, 2½" × 42"; crosscut *10 of the strips* into
    30 strips, 2½" × 10½"

From the red print for binding, cut *on the bias*:

2½"-wide strips to total 310"

Making the Blocks

Press seam allowances in the directions indicated by
the arrows.

1 Referring to "Making Triangle-in-a-Square
Units" on page 6, use the eggshell center
triangles and green side triangles to make 18 sets
of 16 matching triangle units (288 total). Trim each
unit to 2½" square, including seam allowances.

Make 18 sets of 16 matching units,
2½" × 2½".

2 Join two eggshell 1⅞" × 9" strips and one red
print 2" × 9" strip as shown to make a strip set
measuring 4¾" × 9", including seam allowances.
Make 18 strip sets. Cut each strip set into four
1⅞" × 4¾" segments (72 total).

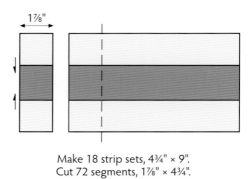

Make 18 strip sets, 4¾" × 9".
Cut 72 segments, 1⅞" × 4¾".

3 Lay out two matching segments from step 3
and one matching red print 2" × 4¾" strip as
shown. Join the pieces to make a cross unit. Make
36 units measuring 4¾" square, including seam
allowances.

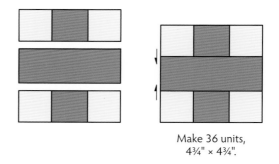

Make 36 units,
4¾" × 4¾".

4 Center and sew matching green triangles to
opposite sides of a cross unit. Sew matching
green triangles to the remaining two sides of the
unit to make a center unit. Trim the unit to 6½"
square, making sure to leave ¼" beyond the points
for seam allowances. Make 36 units.

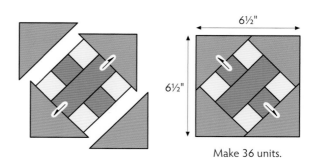

Make 36 units.

Pieced by Anna Dineen and quilted by Carrie Straka

5 Lay out two matching triangle units and three eggshell 2½" squares as shown. Join the units and squares to make a unit measuring 2½" × 10½", including seam allowances. Make 18 sets of four matching top and bottom units (72 total).

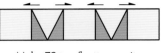

Make 72 top/bottom units,
2½" × 10½".

6 Lay out two matching triangle units and one eggshell 2½" square as shown. Join units and square to make a side unit measuring 2½" × 6½", including seam allowances. Make 18 sets of four matching side units (72 total).

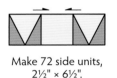

Make 72 side units,
2½" × 6½".

7 Lay out one center unit from step 5, two side units, and two top and bottom units in three rows, making sure the green is the same in all the units. Sew all the pieces into rows and then join the rows. Make 36 blocks measuring 10½" square, including seam allowances.

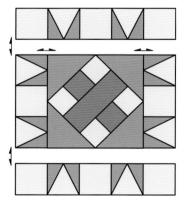

Make 36 blocks,
10½" × 10½".

Assembling the Quilt Top

1 Join six blocks and five ivory 2½" × 10½" strips to make a block row. Make six rows measuring 10½" × 70½", including seam allowances.

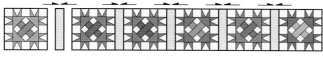

Make 6 rows,
10½" × 70½".

2 Join nine ivory 2½"-wide strips end to end. From the pieced strip, cut five 70½"-long sashing strips.

3 Lay out the block rows and sashing strips, alternating their position as shown in the quilt assembly diagram below. Join the rows and strips to make the quilt-top center, which should measure 70½" square, including seam allowances.

4 Join the remaining ivory 2½"-wide strips end to end. From the pieced strip, cut two 70½"-long strips and sew them to the left and right sides of the quilt top. Cut two 74½"-long strips and sew them to the top and bottom edges. The quilt top should measure 74½"square.

Finishing the Quilt

For more details on any of the finishing steps, go to ShopMartingale.com/HowtoQuilt to download free illustrated information.

1 Layer the quilt top, batting, and backing; baste the layers together.

2 Quilt by hand or machine. The quilt shown is machine quilted with an allover leaf design.

3 Trim the excess batting and backing. Use the red 2½"-wide bias strips to make double-fold binding and attach the binding to the quilt.

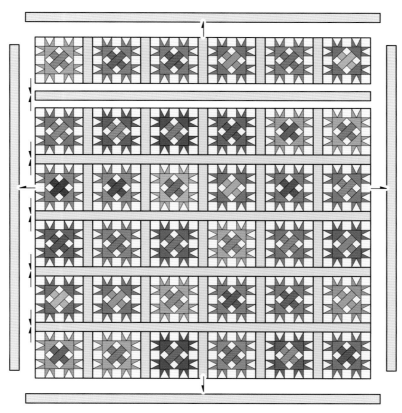

Quilt assembly

Taffy Pull

As a kid, I loved saltwater taffy. Any trip to the beach or to the mountains invariably included a visit to a touristy candy shop, where I'd stand mesmerized in front of the taffy-pulling machine as it stretched and softened the candy. The bright and cheerful fabrics used in this quilt form "twists" that are every bit as sweet as that taffy I used to eat!

Finished quilt: 66" x 80¼"
Finished block: 10" x 10"

Materials

Yardage is based on 42"-wide fabric. Fat eighths measure 9" × 21". Fabric requirements and cutting instructions are for a Tri-Recs Tool set. If you're using a Bloc Loc Ruler Set, increase the amount of ivory solid to 4½ yards.

♦ 32 fat eighths of assorted prints for blocks

♦ 4⅛ yards of ivory solid for block backgrounds, setting triangles, and outer border

♦ ⅝ yard of multicolored floral for inner border

♦ ⅝ yard of teal print for binding

♦ 5 yards of fabric for backing

♦ 74" × 89" piece of batting

♦ Tri-Recs Tool set *OR* 2" × 2" Bloc Loc Triangle in a Square Ruler Set *OR* template plastic

Getting Organized

For this quilt, sort the assorted prints into pairs and label the fabrics as A and B. Each pair will make two blocks. Fabric A will form the outer twist in the first block and the inner twist in the second block. Fabric B will form the inner twist in the first block and the outer twist in the second block.

Sort your fabrics into pairs before cutting and sewing, and then snap a photo of the fabric pairings to have as a ready reference in case the fabrics get out of order during the cutting and sewing process!

Pieced by Anna Dineen and quilted by Amanda Birdwell

You've Got a Point!

Cutting

All measurements include ¼" seam allowances. If you're not using Tri-Recs Tools or a Bloc Loc Triangle in a Square Ruler Set, trace the patterns for the center and side triangles on page 79 onto template plastic and cut them out. Refer to "Cutting the Triangles" on page 9 for detailed instructions as needed.

From *each* of the assorted prints, cut on the *lengthwise grain*:

1 strip, 2½" × 9"; fold the strip in half lengthwise, right sides together, and use a Recs Tool or side triangle template to cut the strip into 4 pairs of side triangles (128 pairs total)

1 strip, 2½" × 9"; crosscut into 2 pieces, 2½" × 4½" (64 total)

1 strip, 2½" × 6½" (32 total)

From the ivory solid, cut:

2 strips, 15½" × 42"; crosscut into:
- 4 squares, 15½" × 15½"; cut the squares in quarters diagonally to yield 16 side triangles (2 are extra)
- 2 squares, 8" × 8"; cut the squares in half diagonally to yield 4 corner triangles

4 strips, 6½" × 42"; crosscut into 64 strips, 2½" × 6½"

4 strips, 4½" × 42"; crosscut into 64 pieces, 2½" × 4½"

8 strips, 3" × 42"

14 strips, 2½" × 42"; crosscut into:

128 center triangles using a Tri Tool or center triangle template

128 squares, 2½" × 2½"

From the multicolored floral, cut:

7 strips, 2½" × 42"

From the teal print, cut *on the bias*:

2½"-wide strips to total 310"

Making the Blocks

Press seam allowances in the directions indicated by the arrows.

1 Select the pieces from one of the assorted prints and label them as A. Select the pieces from a different print and label them B. Each pair of prints will make two blocks.

2 Referring to "Making Triangle-in-a-Square Units" on page 6, use the ivory center triangles and the A and B side triangles to make two sets of four matching units. Trim each unit to 2½" square, including seam allowances.

Make 2 sets of 4 matching units,
2½" × 2½".

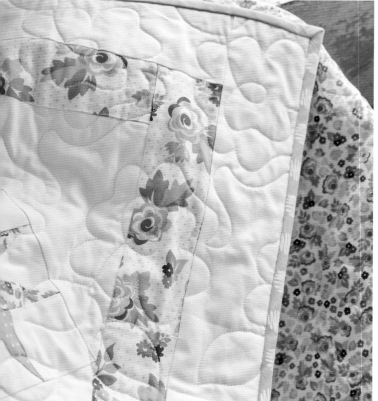

3 Lay out four ivory 2½" squares, two fabric A triangle units, two fabric B triangle units, two fabric B 2½" × 4½" pieces, one fabric A 2½" × 6½" strip, two ivory 2½" × 6½" strips, and two ivory 2½" × 4½" pieces in five rows as shown. Sew all the pieces into rows and then join the rows to make a block. Make a total of 16 A blocks measuring 10½" square, including seam allowances.

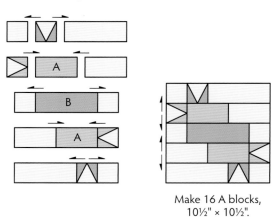

Make 16 A blocks,
10½" × 10½".

4 Repeat steps 2, reversing the positions of the A and B fabrics, to make a total of 16 B blocks measuring 10½" square, including seam allowances.

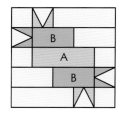

Make 16 B blocks,
10½" × 10½".

Assembling the Quilt Top

1 Referring to the quilt assembly diagram on page 57, arrange and sew the blocks together in diagonal rows, adding the side triangles to the ends of each row as indicated. Join the rows, adding the corner triangles last.

2 Trim and square up the quilt top, making sure to leave ¼" beyond the points of all blocks for seam allowances. The quilt top should measure 57" × 71¼", including seam allowances.

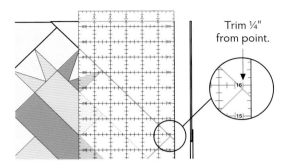

Trim ¼" from point.

3 Join the floral 2½"-wide strips end to end. From the pieced strip, cut two 71¼"-long strips and sew them to the left and right sides of the quilt-top center. Cut two 61"-long strips and sew them to the top and bottom edges. The quilt top should measure 61" × 75¼", including seam allowances.

4 Join the ivory 3" × 42" strips end to end. From the pieced strip, cut two 75¼"-long strips and sew them to the left and right sides of the quilt top. Cut two 66"-long strips and sew them to the top and bottom edges. The quilt top should measure 66" × 80¼".

Finishing the Quilt

For more details on any of the finishing steps, go to ShopMartingale.com/HowtoQuilt to download free illustrated information.

1 Layer the quilt top, batting, and backing; baste the layers together.

2 Quilt by hand or machine. The quilt shown is machine quilted with an allover floral design.

3 Trim the excess batting and backing. Use the teal 2½"-wide bias strips to make double-fold binding and attach the binding to the quilt.

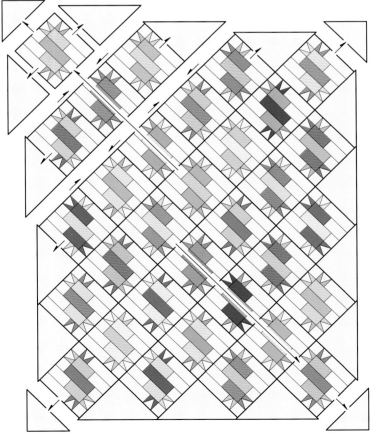

Quilt assembly

Taffy Pull

Spinning Wheels

Spinning Wheels is the answer to the question, What happens when I replace the half-square triangles in a Churn Dash block with triangle-in-a-square units? Set on point, these modified Churn blocks form a lattice around Swamp Angel blocks, reminding me of old-fashioned spinning wheels. Feel free to get scrappy with this pattern—using lots of different prints adds interest to the two-color design.

Finished quilt: 64" × 77"

Finished block: 9" × 9"

Materials

Yardage is based on 42"-wide fabric. Fat quarters measure 18" × 22". Fabric requirements and cutting instructions are based on using a Tri-Recs Tool set. If you're using a Bloc Loc Ruler Set, you'll need to increase the amount of fabric for the triangle units by about 25% (15 fat quarters of red prints and 5¼ yards of ivory solid).

♦ 4½ yards of ivory solid for blocks and setting triangles

♦ 12 fat quarters of assorted red prints for blocks

♦ 12 fat quarters of assorted aqua prints for blocks

♦ ⅝ yard of red check for binding

♦ 4⅝ yards of fabric for backing

♦ 70" × 83" piece of batting

♦ Tri-Recs Tool set *OR* 3" × 3" Bloc Loc Triangle in a Square Ruler Set *OR* template plastic

Cutting

All measurements include ¼" seam allowances. If you're not using Tri-Recs Tools or a Bloc Loc Triangle in a Square Ruler Set, trace the patterns for the center and side triangles on page 79 onto template plastic and cut them out. Refer to "Cutting the Triangles" on page 9 for detailed instructions as needed.

From the ivory solid, cut:

3 strips, 14" × 42"; crosscut into:

  5 squares, 14" × 14"; cut the squares into quarters diagonally to yield 20 side triangles (2 are extra)

  2 squares, 7¼" × 7¼"; cut the squares in half diagonally to yield 4 corner triangles

5 strips, 4½" × 42"; crosscut into 40 squares, 4½" × 4½". Cut the squares in half diagonally to yield 80 triangles.

4 strips, 4" × 42"; crosscut into 40 squares, 4" × 4". Cut the squares in half diagonally to yield 80 triangles.

19 strips, 3½" × 42"; crosscut into:
  • 12 strips, 3½" × 18"
  • 72 squares, 3½" × 3½"
  • 120 pieces, 2" × 3½"

Continued on page 60

Continued from page 59

From *each* of the red prints, cut on the *lengthwise* grain:

3 strips, 3½" × 18"; crosscut *2 of the strips* into 10 pieces, 2" × 3½" (120 total)

1 square, 2" × 2" (24 total; 2 are extra)

From *each* of 11 red prints, cut on the *lengthwise* grain:

2 strips, 3½" × 18"; use a Tri Tool or center triangle template to cut the strips into 9 center triangles (99 total; 1 is extra)

From *each* of 6 aqua prints, cut:

1 strip, 4½" × 21"; crosscut into 4 squares, 4½" × 4½". Cut the squares in half diagonally to yield 8 triangles (48 total).

1 strip, 4" × 21"; crosscut into 4 squares, 4" × 4". Cut the squares in half diagonally to yield 8 triangles (48 total).

From *each* of the remaining 6 aqua prints, cut:

1 strip, 4½" × 21"; crosscut into 3 squares, 4½" × 4½". Cut the squares in half diagonally to yield 6 triangles (36 total; 4 are extra).

1 strip, 4" × 21"; crosscut into 3 squares, 4" × 4". Cut the squares in half diagonally to yield 6 triangles (36 total; 4 are extra).

From the red check, cut *on the bias*:

2½"-wide strips to total 300"

Making the Churn Blocks

Press seam allowances in the directions indicated by the arrows.

1 Layer one ivory and one red 3½" × 18" strip right sides together with the ivory strip on top. Referring to "Cutting the Triangles" on page 9, use a Recs Tool or side triangle template to crosscut into 98 pairs of side triangles (the right-side triangles will be red and the left-side triangles will be ivory).

2 Referring to "Making Triangle-in-a-Square Units" on page 6, use the red center triangles, red right-side triangles, and ivory left-side triangles

to make 98 triangle units. Trim each unit to 3½" square, including seam allowances.

Make 98 units, 3½" × 3½".

Make It Scrappy

Feel free to mix up the red prints as you make your triangle-in-a-square units—the prints for the center triangle and right-side triangle don't have to match! This is a great way to make your blocks look extra scrappy.

3 Draw a diagonal line from corner to corner on the wrong side of the red 2" square. Layer a marked square on one corner of an ivory 3½" square, right sides together. Sew on the marked line. Trim the excess corner fabric ¼" from the stitched line to make a corner unit. Make 22 units measuring 3½" square, including seam allowances.

Make 22 corner units, 3½" × 3½".

4 Join a red and an ivory 2" × 3½" piece to make a bar unit. Make 120 units measuring 3½" square, including seam allowances.

Make 120 bar units, 3½" × 3½".

Pieced by Anna Dineen and quilted by Carrie Straka

5 Lay out two corner units, two triangle units, four bar units, and one ivory 3½" square in three rows as shown. Sew all the pieces into rows. Join the rows to make a corner Churn block. Make four blocks measuring 9½" square, including seam allowances.

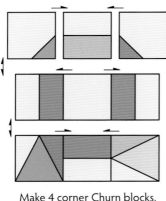

Make 4 corner Churn blocks,
9½" × 9½".

6 Lay out three triangle units, one corner unit, four bar units, and one ivory 3½" square in three rows as shown. Sew all the pieces into rows. Join the rows to make a side Churn block. Make 14 blocks measuring 9½" square, including seam allowances.

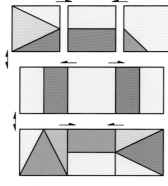

Make 14 side Churn blocks,
9½" × 9½".

7 Lay out four triangle units, four bar units, and one ivory 3½" square in three rows as shown. Sew all the pieces into rows. Join the rows to make a center Churn block. Make 12 blocks measuring 9½" square, including seam allowances.

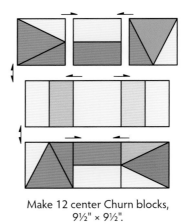

Make 12 center Churn blocks,
9½" × 9½".

Making the Swamp Angel Blocks

1 Layer an aqua and an ivory 4" triangle right sides together and sew along the bias edge to make a half-square-triangle unit. Trim the unit to 3½" square, including seam allowances. Make 80 units.

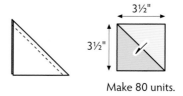

Make 80 units.

2 Layer an aqua and an ivory 4½" triangle right sides together and sew along the bias edge to make a half-square-triangle unit. Make 80 units measuring 4⅛" square, including seam allowances.

Make 80 units,
4⅛" × 4⅛".

3 Cut each half-square-triangle unit from step 2 in half diagonally to make two quarter-triangle units. Layer two quarter-triangle units right sides together, making sure contrasting fabrics are facing each other. Butt the seams against each other. Sew along the bias edge to make an hourglass unit. Trim each unit to 3½" square, including seam allowances. Make 80 units.

Make 80 units.

Mix It Up

As you make the hourglass units, pair up quarter-triangle units with different aqua prints for another opportunity to boost the scrappiness-factor of your quilt.

4 Lay out four half-square-triangle units, four hourglass units, and one ivory 3½" square in three rows as shown. Sew all the pieces into rows. Join the rows to make a Swamp Angel block. Make 20 blocks measuring 9½" square, including seam allowances.

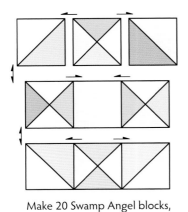

Make 20 Swamp Angel blocks, 9½" × 9½".

Assembling the Quilt Top

1 Referring to the quilt assembly diagram below, arrange and sew the Churn and Swamp Angel blocks together in diagonal rows, adding the side triangles to the ends of each row as indicated. Join the rows, adding the corner triangles last.

2 Trim and square up the quilt top, making sure to leave ¼" beyond the points of all blocks for seam allowances. The quilt top should measure 64" × 77".

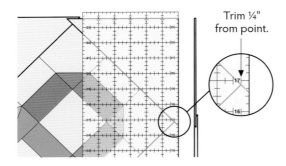

Trim ¼" from point.

3 Stitch around the perimeter of the quilt top, ⅛" from the outer edges, to lock the seams in place.

Finishing the Quilt

For more details on any of the finishing steps, go to ShopMartingale.com/HowtoQuilt to download free illustrated information.

1 Layer the quilt top, batting, and backing; baste the layers together.

2 Quilt by hand or machine. The quilt shown is machine quilted with an allover swirl pattern.

3 You can leave the quilt square, or round the corners as I did. To round the corners, place a round plate or cardboard circle on each corner triangle and trace the curve. Trim the corner on the drawn line.

4 Trim the excess batting and backing. Use the red check 2½"-wide bias strips to make double-fold binding and attach the binding to the quilt.

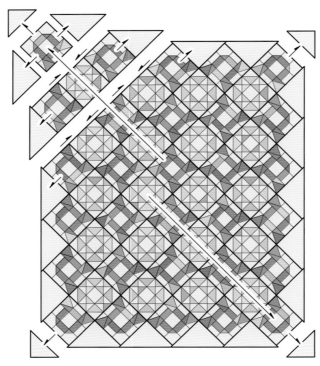

Quilt assembly

You've Got a Point!

Queens Road

Queens Road winds through a lovely historic neighborhood in Charlotte, North Carolina, my hometown. It's a wide, tree-lined boulevard where you can find quaint Tudor homes nestled between stately Colonials. I've always been enamored with the architectural details of Tudor homes, especially the half-timber framing and tall windows with diamond-shaped panes. I used those details as inspiration for this design, my homage to the beautiful city where I grew up.

Finished quilt:
63½" × 65"

Finished blocks:
4½" × 4½" and 4½" × 9"

Materials

Yardage is based on 42"-wide fabric. Fat quarters measure 18" × 21".

♦ 2½ yards of light blue solid for blocks, sashing, and inner border
♦ 2¾ yards of porcelain solid for blocks
♦ 18 fat quarters of assorted prints for blocks
♦ ¾ yard of blue floral for outer border
♦ ⅝ yard of red floral for binding
♦ 4 yards of fabric for backing
♦ 70" × 71" piece of batting
♦ 4" × 4" Bloc Loc Triangle in a Square Ruler Set *OR* template plastic

Cutting

All measurements include ¼" seam allowances. If you're not using a Bloc Loc Triangle in a Square Ruler Set, trace the patterns for the center and side triangles on page 71 onto template plastic and cut them out.

From the light blue solid, cut:
4 strips, 5½" × 42"; crosscut into 144 strips, 1" × 5½"
24 strips, 2" × 42"; crosscut *16 of the strips* into 16 strips, 2" × 27½"
8 strips, 1⅜" × 42"

Continued on page 67

Continued from page 65

From the porcelain solid, cut:

8 strips, 5⅛" × 42"; keeping strips folded in half with selvedge edges together, use the Bloc Loc side triangle template or plastic template to cut the strips into 72 pairs of side triangles

6 strips, 1⅜" × 42"

4 strips, 2" × 42"

9 strips, 3½" × 42"; crosscut into 96 squares, 3½" × 3½". Cut the squares in half diagonally to yield 192 triangles.

From *each* of the assorted prints, cut:

2 pieces, 5½" × 10½" (36 total)

From the blue floral, cut:

7 strips, 3½" × 42"

From the red floral, cut *on the bias*:

2½"-wide strips to total 275"

Making the Checkerboard Blocks

Press seam allowances in the directions indicated by the arrows.

1 Join two light blue 1⅜" × 42" strips and one porcelain 2" × 42" strip as shown to make strip set A. Make four strip sets measuring 3¾" × 42", including seam allowances. Cut the strip sets into 96 A segments, 1⅜" × 3¾".

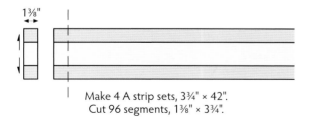

Make 4 A strip sets, 3¾" × 42".
Cut 96 segments, 1⅜" × 3¾".

2 Join two porcelain 1⅜" × 42" strips and one light blue 2" × 42" strip as shown to make strip set B. Make three strip sets measuring 3¾" × 42", including seam allowances. Cut the strip sets into 48 B segments, 2" × 3¾".

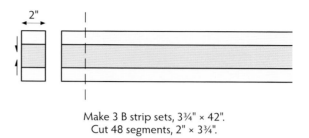

Make 3 B strip sets, 3¾" × 42".
Cut 48 segments, 2" × 3¾".

3 Join two A segments and one B segment to make a nine-patch unit. Make 48 units measuring 3¾" square, including seam allowances.

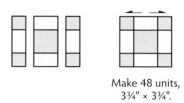

Make 48 units,
3¾" × 3¾".

4 Center and sew porcelain 3½" triangles to opposite sides of a nine-patch unit. Sew porcelain 3½" triangles to the remaining two sides of the unit, as shown, to make a block. Trim the block to 5" square, making sure to leave ¼" beyond the points for seam allowances Make 48 Checkerboard blocks.

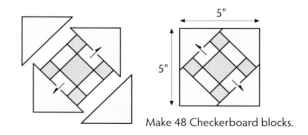

Make 48 Checkerboard blocks.

Pieced by Anna Dineen and quilted by Carrie Straka

You've Got a Point!

Making the Diamond Blocks

1 Fold a print 5½" × 10½" piece in half so it's 5½" × 5¼". Align the bottom of the Bloc Loc center triangle template or a plastic template with the fold. Cut along the left and right sides of the triangle template only to release a diamond. Repeat to cut a total of 36 diamonds.

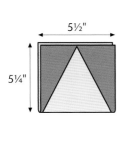

Make 36 diamonds.

2 Fold a light blue 1" × 5½" rectangle in half lengthwise and press to make a frame strip that measures ½" × 5½". Make 144 frame strips.

3 Place frame strips on opposite edges of a diamond, aligning the raw edges of the frame strips with the edges of the diamond. Increase the stitch length on your machine and baste the frame strips to the diamond using a ⅛" seam allowance. Repeat to baste frame strips on the remaining edges of the diamond. Make 36 framed diamonds.

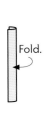
Fold.
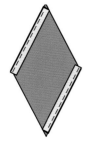

4 Referring to "Stitching the Triangles" on page 11, sew porcelain side triangles to opposite sides of a framed diamond. Sew porcelain side triangles to the remaining sides of the diamond to make a

Windowpane block. Make 36 blocks and trim them to measure 5" × 9½", including seam allowances.

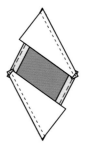
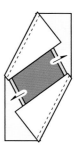

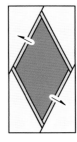

Make 36 Windowpane blocks, 5" × 9½".

Assembling the Quilt Top

1 Join six Checkerboard blocks to make a column measuring 5" × 27½", including seam allowances. Sew light blue 2" × 27½" strips to opposite sides of the column to make a Checkerboard column. Make eight columns measuring 8" × 27½", including seam allowances.

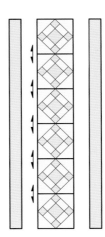
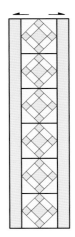

Make 8 Checkerboard columns, 8" × 27½".

2 Lay out six Windowpane blocks in three rows of two blocks each. Sew the blocks into rows and then join the rows to make a Windowpane column. Make six columns measuring 9½" × 27½", including seam allowances.

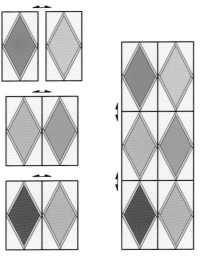

Make 6 Windowpane columns,
9½" × 27½".

3 Join four Checkerboard columns and three Windowpane columns to make the top section, which should measure 57½" × 27½", including seam allowances. Repeat to make the bottom section.

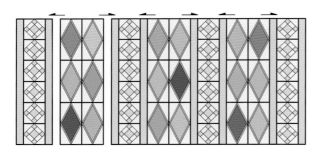

Make 2 sections,
57½" × 27½".

4 Join the remaining blue solid 2"-wide strips end to end. From the pieced strip, cut three 57½"-long strips.

5 Referring to the quilt assembly diagram below, join the sections from step 3 and the blue strips from step 4 to make the quilt-top center. The quilt top should measure 57½" × 59", including seam allowances.

6 Join the blue floral 3½"-wide strips end to end. From the pieced strip, cut two 59"-long strips and sew them to the left and right sides of the quilt top. Cut two 63½"-long strips and sew them to the top and bottom edges. The quilt top should measure 63½" × 65".

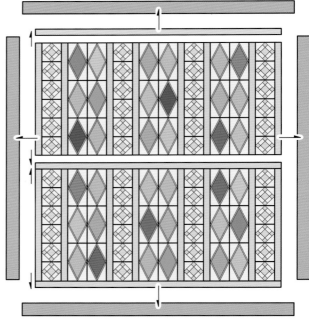

Quilt assembly

Finishing the Quilt

For more details on any of the finishing steps, go to ShopMartingale.com/HowtoQuilt to download free illustrated information.

1 Layer the quilt top, batting, and backing; baste the layers together.

2 Quilt by hand or machine. The quilt shown is machine quilted with an allover swirl design.

3 Trim the excess batting and backing. Use the red floral 2½"-wide bias strips to make double-fold binding and attach the binding to the quilt.

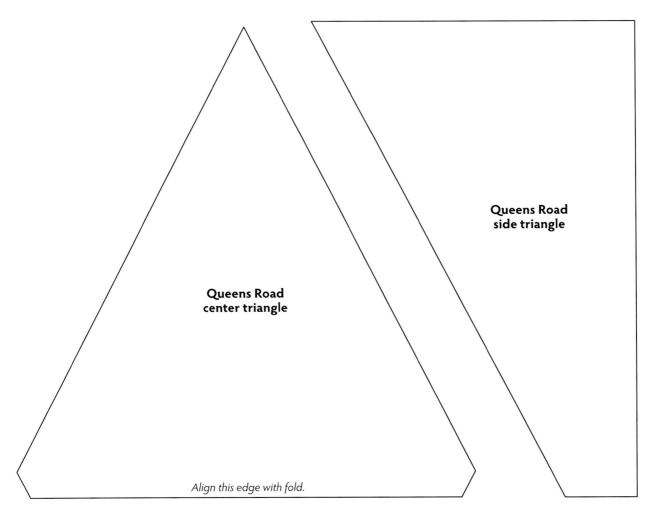

Queens Road center triangle

Queens Road side triangle

Align this edge with fold.

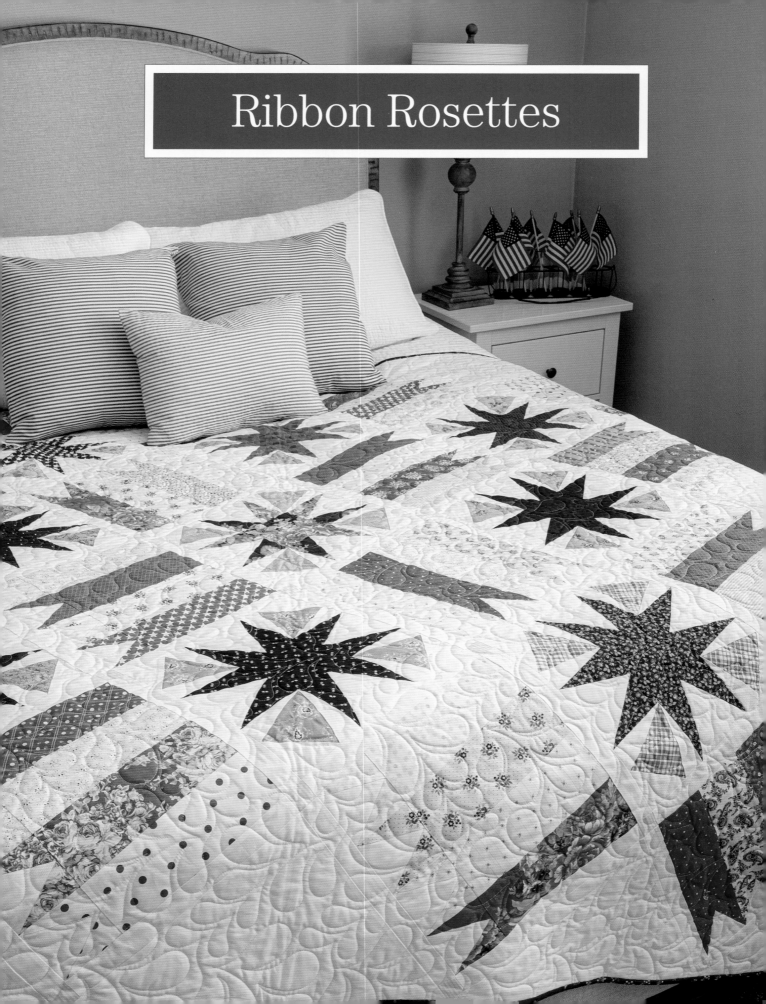

Ribbon Rosettes

I love patriotic quilts and just had to include one in this book. As I was working on possible designs, I couldn't stop thinking about those giant county-fair-style prize ribbons. Pairing triangle-in-a-square units with long rectangles mimics ribbon tails, while stars set on point make Maltese Cross rosettes. Put together, the ribbons and rosettes create an irresistibly festive, summery design that offers a fresh take on the classic patriotic quilt.

Finished quilt: 75½" × 75½"
Finished block: 12" × 12"

Materials

Yardage is based on 42"-wide fabric. Fat eighths measure 9" × 21". Fabric requirements and cutting instructions are for a Tri-Recs Tool set. If you're using a Bloc Loc Ruler Set, increase the amount of ivory solid to 5¼ yards.

- 4⅝ yards of ivory solid for blocks, sashing, and setting triangles
- 9 fat eighths of assorted blue prints for Rosette blocks
- 9 fat eighths of assorted navy prints for Rosette blocks
- 16 fat eighths of assorted red and pink prints for Ribbon blocks
- 16 fat eighths of assorted light prints for Ribbon blocks
- 1 fat eighth of tan print for cornerstones
- ⅝ yard of navy print for binding
- 6⅞ yards of fabric for backing
- 82" × 82" piece of batting
- Newsprint for foundation piecing
- Tri-Recs Tool set *OR* 4" × 4" and 3" × 3" Bloc Loc Triangle in a Square Ruler Sets *OR* template plastic

Cutting

All measurements include ¼" seam allowances. If you're not using Tri-Recs Tools or a Bloc Loc Triangle in a Square Ruler Set, trace the patterns for the center and side triangles on page 79 onto template plastic and cut them out. Refer to "Cutting the Triangles" on page 9 for detailed instructions as needed.

From *each* of the navy prints, cut *on the lengthwise grain*:

2 strips, 4½" × 9"; fold strips in half, right sides together, and use a Recs Tool or side triangle template to cut the strips into 4 pairs of side triangles (36 pairs total)

1 square, 4½" × 4½" (9 total)

From *each* of the blue prints, cut:

1 strip, 4½" × 21"; crosscut into 4 squares, 4½" × 4½" (36 total)

Continued on page 74

Continued from page 73

From the ivory solid, cut:

2 strips, 20" × 42"; crosscut into 3 squares, 20" × 20". Cut the squares into quarters diagonally to yield 12 side setting triangles.

1 strip, 11" × 42"; crosscut into 2 squares, 11" × 11". Cut the squares in half diagonally to yield 4 corner setting triangles.

7 strips, 5½" × 42"; crosscut into:
- 72 pieces, 2½" × 5½"
- 36 rectangles, 3" × 5½"

3 strips, 4½" × 42"; use a Tri Tool or center triangle template to cut the strips into 36 center triangles

4 strips, 3½" × 42"; use a Tri Tool or center triangle template to cut the strips into 64 center triangles

22 strips, 1½" × 42"; crosscut into 64 strips, 1½" × 12½"

From *each* of the red and pink prints, cut:

1 strip, 3½" × 21"; crosscut into 2 strips, 3½" × 9½" (32 total)

1 strip, 3½" × 21"; fold the strip in half, right sides together, and use a Recs Tool or side triangle template to cut the strip into 2 pairs of side triangles (32 pairs total)

From *each* of the light prints, cut:

1 strip, 3½" × 21"; crosscut into 2 strips, 3½" × 9½" (32 total)

1 strip, 3½" × 21"; fold the strip in half, right sides together, and use a Recs Tool or side triangle template to cut the strip into 2 pairs of side triangles (32 pairs total)

From the ecru print, cut:

4 strips, 1½" × 21"; crosscut into 40 squares, 1½" × 1½"

From the navy print for binding, cut *on the bias*:

2½"-wide strips to total 334"

Making the Rosette Blocks

Press seam allowances in the directions indicated by the arrows.

1 Make 36 copies of the foundation pattern on page 78.

2 Referring to "Paper-Foundation Piecing" on page 13, paper piece nine sets of four matching triangle units (36 total) as follows:

- Piece 1: blue 4½" square
- Pieces 2 and 3: ivory 2½" × 5½" pieces
- Piece 4: ivory 3" × 5½" piece

Make 9 sets of 4 matching units,
4½" × 4½".

3 Referring to "Stitching the Triangles" on page 11, use the ivory 4½" center triangles and navy side triangles to make nine sets of four matching triangle units (36 total). Trim each unit to 4½" square, including seam allowances.

Make 9 sets of 4 matching units,
4½" × 4½".

4 Lay out four matching units from step 1, four matching units from step 2, and one navy 4½" square in three rows. The navy print should be the same throughout. Sew the units into rows and then join the rows to make a Rosette block. Make nine blocks measuring 12½" square, including seam allowances.

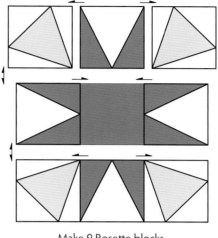

Make 9 Rosette blocks,
12½" × 12½".

Making the Ribbon Blocks

1 Referring to "Making Triangle-in-a-Square Units" and using an ivory 3½" center triangle and two matching red or pink side triangles, make 32 red or pink triangle units. Trim each unit to 3½" square, including seam allowances. Repeat to make 32 light units.

Make 32 units,   Make 32 units,
3½" × 3½".   3½" × 3½".

2 Sew a triangle unit to the end of a matching red or pink 3½" × 9½" strip to make a ribbon unit. Make 32 red or pink ribbon units measuring 3½" × 12½", including seam allowances. Repeat to make 32 light ribbon units.

Make 32 units,   Make 32 units,
3½" × 12½".   3½" × 12½".

Pieced by Anna Dineen and quilted by Carrie Straka

You've Got a Point!

3 Lay out two different red or pink ribbon units and two different light ribbon units, alternating their positions as shown. Join the units to make a Ribbon block. Make 10 blocks measuring 12½" square, including seam allowances. Repeat to make six mirror-image Ribbon blocks.

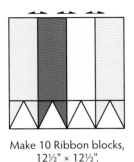

Make 10 Ribbon blocks,
12½" × 12½".

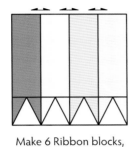

Make 6 Ribbon blocks,
12½" × 12½".

Assembling the Quilt Top

1 Referring to the quilt assembly diagram below, lay out the blocks, ivory 1½" × 12½" strips, tan squares, and ivory side and corner triangles in diagonal rows. Join the ivory strips and tan squares to make sashing rows. Sew the blocks and ivory strips into rows to make block rows. Sew a sashing row to the top or bottom of each appropriate block row, and then add the side triangles. Join the rows, adding the corner triangles last.

2 Trim and square up the quilt top, making sure to leave ¼" beyond the points of all the tan squares for seam allowances. The quilt top should measure 75½" square. including seam allowances.

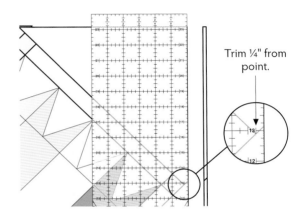

Trim ¼" from
point.

3 Stitch around the perimeter of the quilt top, ⅛" from the outer edges, to lock the seams in place.

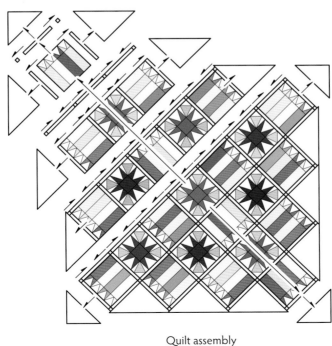

Quilt assembly

Divide and Conquer

When sewing the rows of my quilts together, especially when I'm working with an on-point setting, I treat the middle row as the dividing line between the top and bottom halves of the quilt and work my way out from there. For Ribbon Rosettes, I sewed a sashing row to both sides of the middle row and set it aside. Then I joined rows 3, 2, and 1 (in that order) to form the top half, and sewed rows 5, 6, and 7 to form the bottom half. I always press the seam allowances toward the smaller row. I joined the middle row to the top half first, pressing the seam allowances toward row 3, and finally, I joined the two halves together and pressed toward row 5.

Finishing the Quilt

For more details on any of the finishing steps, go to ShopMartingale.com/HowtoQuilt to download free illustrated information.

1 Layer the quilt top, batting, and backing; baste the layers together.

2 Quilt by hand or machine. The quilt shown is machine quilted with an allover feather design.

3 Trim the excess batting and backing. Use the navy 2½"-wide bias strips to make double-fold binding and attach the binding to the quilt.

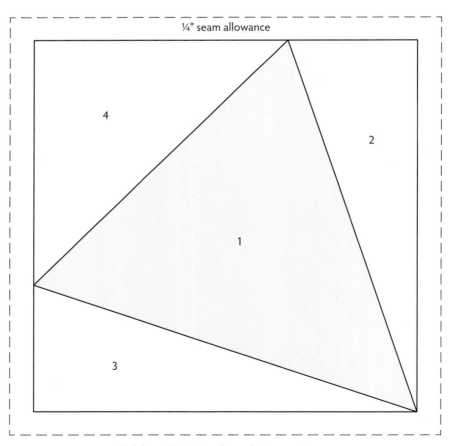

Ribbon Rosettes foundation pattern
Make 36 copies.

You've Got a Point!

Triangle Patterns

In this section, you'll find triangle patterns to make all of the projects in this book except Queens Road. You'll need one template for each triangle. To make a template, place a piece of template plastic over the required pattern. Use a fine-tip permanent marker to trace the line of the shape exactly onto the plastic, making sure to use the correct line for the project you're making. Then use utility scissors to cut out the template *exactly* on the drawn line.

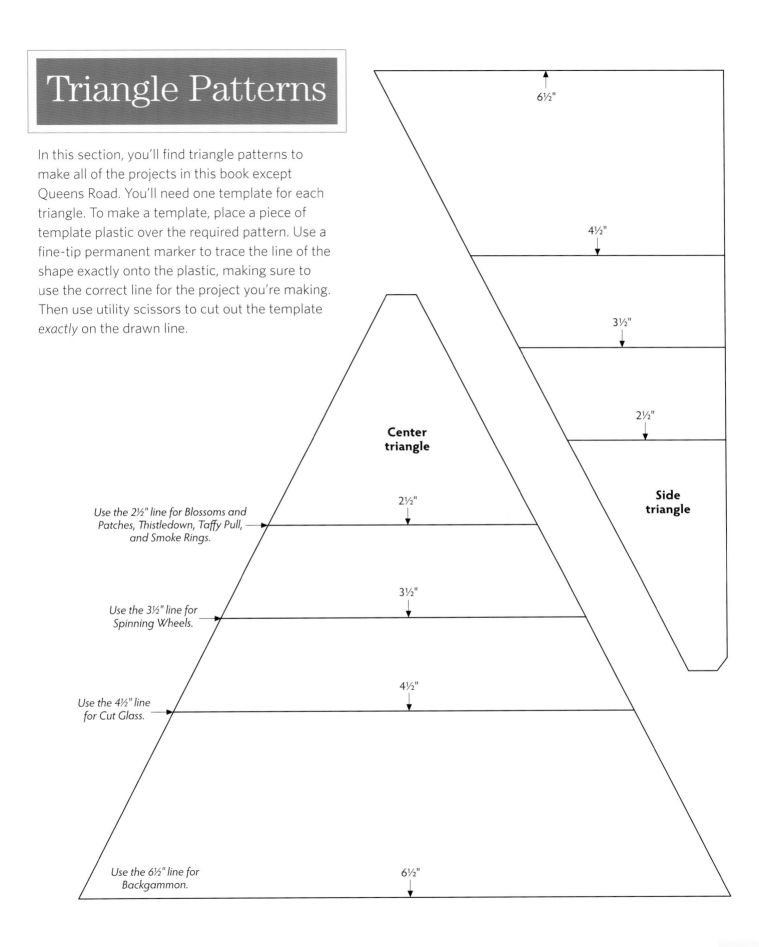

6½"

4½"

3½"

2½"

Side triangle

Center triangle

2½"

Use the 2½" line for Blossoms and Patches, Thistledown, Taffy Pull, and Smoke Rings.

3½"

Use the 3½" line for Spinning Wheels.

4½"

Use the 4½" line for Cut Glass.

6½"

Use the 6½" line for Backgammon.

Acknowledgements

Writing a quilt book is not a solitary endeavor! I have been helped, cheered on, and supported during this process in so many ways by an amazing group of people.

I am incredibly grateful for the three loves of my life: my husband, Guy, and my children, Uma Claire and Ethan. Thank you for showering me with love and grace as I embarked on this new chapter of my quilting journey.

I'm so lucky to have a loving and supportive family. Thank you Mom, Daddy, Claire Lee, and the extended Hayes/Porter crew for encouraging me to follow my dreams and helping me become the person I am today.

Thank you to my soul sisters, Rebecca Kiessling, Amy Hickox, and Melanie Reeve, for the gift of your friendship, love, support, and laughter.

I can't thank Martingale enough for believing in my vision for this book and for helping me bring it to life. It has been a pleasure to work with you all, especially Beth Kovich and Karen Soltys.

Thanks to my friends at Moda Fabrics for so generously providing fabric for this book! I'm especially indebted to Lissa Alexander, Carrie Nelson, and Joanna Figueroa for teaching, encouraging, and inspiring me. Each of you has opened doors of opportunity for me and I'm forever grateful.

To my quilty friends Sarah Gozzo, Judy Kirby, Karen O'Connor, and Kim Strickler: Thank you for your pattern feedback, your wise counsel, and for just being wonderful people in general. Your friendships have buoyed my spirits on countless occasions.

A quilt top becomes something extraordinary with a talented long-arm quilter's touch. To Amanda Birdwell, Maggi Honeyman, and Carrie Straka, thank you for the skill and artistry that you brought to the quilts in this book and for being so wonderful to work with!

Special thanks to Mary Andra Holmes, whose quick and impeccable stitching skills helped me cross the finish line! Finally, to the online quilting community: The path that led to this book began the day I created my Instagram account and connected with this creative, vibrant community. Thanks to all of you for following along with me on my wandering path.

About the Author

Anna Dineen calls herself a lifelong "serial crafter" who has dabbled in just about every craft that involves a needle and thread, paper and glue, or textiles of any kind. Her crafting career began in 2011, when she combined her love of paper crafting and her entrepreneurial spirit to renovate a turn-of-the-century home into a luxury crafting retreat center.

But the happiest chapter of Anna's creative journey started in 2016, when she began quilting in earnest and launched her blog and Instagram account. Since then, she's worked in the marketing department for a major fabric manufacturer; sewn countless projects for quilt markets, blog tours, and quilting books; contributed to a Moda All-Stars book; and continues to freelance in social media for creative businesswomen.

You can follow Anna on her creative journey at @mywanderingpath and www.mywanderingpath.com.